BOX
BOTTLE
BAG

BOX
BOTTLE
BAG

ANDREW GIBBS

the world's best packaging design from thedieline.com

HOW
BOOKS
Cincinnati, Ohio
www.howdesign.com

For more excellent books and resources for designers, visit www.howdesign.com.

14 13 12 11   5 4 3 2

Distributed in Canada by Fraser Direct
100 Armstrong Avenue
Georgetown, Ontario, Canada L7G 5S4
Tel: (905) 877-4411

Distributed in the U.K. and Europe by David & Charles
Brunel House, Newton Abbot, Devon, TQ12 4PU, England
Tel: (+44) 1626-323200, Fax: (+44) 1626-323319
E-mail: postmaster@davidandcharles.co.uk

Distributed in Australia by Capricorn Link
P.O. Box 704, Windsor, NSW 2756 Australia
Tel: (02) 4577-3555

Library of Congress Cataloging-in-Publication Data

Gibbs, Andrew, 1985-
  Box, bottle, bag / Andrew Gibbs. -- 1st ed.
       p. cm.
  Includes index.
  ISBN 978-1-60061-419-4 (hardcover : alk. paper)
  1. Packaging--Design. I. Title.
  TS195.4.G53 2010
  688.8--dc22
                       2009042999

EDITED BY Amy Schell
DESIGNED BY Grace Ring
PRODUCTION COORDINATED BY Greg Nock

ABOUT THE AUTHOR

Andrew Gibbs founded The Dieline in 2007 and has tended to its growth since then. Andrew has an obvious passion for package design and a strong drive to succeed. He graduated high school at the age of 16, and received his bachelor's degree in graphic design from The Art Institute of California at the age of 19.

Over the course of his short but successful career, he has designed and developed consumer brands and retail packaging for national and international brands, as well as private labels. He currently dedicates his time to running The Dieline, and to his role as creative director for one of the nation's leading beverage development companies, overseeing branding and packaging for new beverage brands.

He resides in Los Angeles, California, with his partner and two crazy cats.

ABOUT THE DIELINE

Established in 2007, TheDieline.com is dedicated to the progress of the package design industry and its practitioners, students and enthusiasts. Its purpose is to define and promote the world's best examples of packaging, and to provide a place where the package design community can review, critique, be inspired and stay informed of the latest industry trends, news and projects being created in the field.

It all started as a weekend project. As a package designer, I wanted a website where I could stay up-to-date with the industry, and be inspired by the best package designs from around the world. When I realized one didn't exist, The Dieline was born. The Dieline's name comes from the printing term "dieline," a precise drawing used as a template for cutting printed materials. As most packaging is printed flat, the dieline forms the complete three dimensional shape of the package, flaps, folds, panels, and even label shapes.

The Dieline has quickly grown into the most visited website on package design in the world, and it has become the voice of the industry. It is used as a daily resource for hundreds of thousands of people around the world. As The Dieline continues to find and define the world's best packaging, we have launched The Dieline Awards, an international design competition recognizing best in package design, further promoting the progress of package design industry.

The Dieline, and everything we do, is for the benefit of our readers. We hope that our efforts and enthusiasm about packaging have inspired you!

TABLE OF
CONTENTS

INTRODUCTION

Have you ever been influenced to buy something solely because of its packaging?
I have. We all have. Packaging plays more of a role in your purchasing decision
than you may think. Think of how many things in your house you bought because
they looked good, not because you really needed them. Well-designed packaging has the power to turn a want into a need, and into a purchase. The thought,
the concept, the ideas, the colors, the shape, the type and all the elements of a
well-designed package work together to create something more than just a product. Great packaging adds more than just monetary value to a product—it adds
emotional value. It has the power to directly trigger the emotions of the consumer,
and it is what makes someone fall in love with a product, or even hate it. It's that
emotional connection that makes a design a success.

The packaging featured in this book has been collected from around the
world over the past two years, since the inception of The Dieline. It is the best of
the best. Instead of being organized by industry or type of packaging, the book is
organized by style. It contains six distinct styles that represent the current state
of the package design industry. Enjoy!

—ANDREW GIBBS

CHAPTER 1
LUXE

LUXE: LUXURIOUS, ELEGANT, LAVISH, OPULENT, REFINED, PREMIUM. THIS SECTION IS ALL ABOUT PACKAGING THAT DEMANDS A PREMIUM (OR AT LEAST LOOKS LIKE IT DOES).

"Trillium is only the second absinthe made in America since the ban of it in 1912. It's made in the traditional French absinthe style, but with the inventiveness that any small-batch distillery brings to a fine spirit. And so the bottle and labeling needs to affirm both that this is, in fact, real absinthe, and yet also that it is the product of the imagination of two young distillers in Portland, Oregon, and of their desire to bring something to the art of absinthe. The floral illustrations depict the actual botanicals used in the making of Trillium."

—ID BRANDING

Integrity Spirits

PORTLAND
OREGON

HAND
CRAFTED

SMALL
BATCH

60%

INTEGRITY SPIRITS

TRILLIUM

ABSINTHE SUPÉRIEURE

750 ML
60% ALC/VOL (120 PROOF)
GRAIN NEUTRAL SPIRITS DISTILLED WITH HERBS

TRILLIUM ABSINTHE

PROJECT: Trillium Absinthe DESIGN FIRM: ID Branding CLIENT: Integrity Spirits DESIGNER: Lily Chow ART DIRECTOR: Jared Milam COPYWRITER: Charla Adams FONTS USED: Custom

SNOWBERRY

PROJECT: Snowberry packaging **DESIGN FIRM:** Interbrand **CLIENT:** Endue Ltd
Design **DESIGNER:** Fiona Fry **CREATIVE DIRECTOR:** Debbie Hyde
EXECUTIVE CREATIVE DIRECTOR: Brad Green **ILLUSTRATOR:** Rob Ryan
FONT USED: Futura

"The design of the Snowberry range of packaging is intended to instantly convey the core ideas of purity, freshness, innocence and enchantment. The name has been incorporated in a block logo to give balance to its inherent gentleness, while the use of white throughout adds to the look of pureness. We commissioned London artist Rob Ryan to create the unique artwork that is Snowberry's visual signature. It is multilayered and tells stories within stories that reflect the Snowberry philosophy. Different parts of the illustration have been used on products throughout the range to make product differentiation easy and to provide a fluid, unexpected nature to the packaging. The use of matte laminate and gloss finishes gives the range a sense of sophistication and style."

—INTERBRAND

IMMUNO-VIVA

PROJECT: Immuno-Viva **DESIGN FIRM:** Zeus Jones **CLIENT:** Botanic Oil Innovations **DESIGNER:** Brad Surcey **ART DIRECTOR:** Brad Surcey **PHOTOGRAPHER:** Chad Hancock **COPYWRITER:** Eric Frost **FONT USED:** Gotham Rounded

"In a category littered with white plastic bottles and pastel color gradients, we decided to design something bold, straightforward and easy to understand."

—ZEUS JONES

"Turner Duckworth was asked to create an identity for a range of Mediterranean products (olive oils, olives, vinegars) that communicated premium brand values targeted at 'foodies' who only use the highest-quality ingredients. The outcome is a design that communicates the handpicked, hand-selected care given to the creation of each product in the range. The symbol shows a hand appearing from the earth as an olive tree icon, while the colors evoke the feeling of the Mediterranean without over-claiming its provenance."

—TURNER DUCKWORTH

PROJECT: Belazu DESIGN FIRM: Turner Duckworth (London & San Francisco) CLIENT: The Fresh Olive Company CREATIVE DIRECTORS: David Turner, Bruce Duckworth DESIGNERS: Janice Davison, Christian Eager FONTS USED: Trade Gothic, ITC Novarese, Gill Sans, Berthold Akzidenz-Grotesk

BELAZU

479° POPCORN

PROJECT: 479° Popcorn **DESIGN FIRM:** The Engine Room **CLIENT:** 479°
Popcorn **DESIGNER:** Dave Braden **ART DIRECTORS:** Dave Braden, Mike
Cotsifas **PHOTOGRAPHER:** Susan Burdick **COPYWRITER:** Jennifer Jeffrey

"We created the identity and packaging for 479° Popcorn—a gourmet, organic popcorn made in small batches using heavy copper kettles. Our challenge was to create an artisan yet urban, chic and fashion-conscious brand identity that would target sophisticated snackers. The solution was rich yet minimal. Large, iconic images of each flavor dominate the ID, an array of color and textile patterns were used to support the flavors, and the shipping boxes were designed to double as gift boxes."

—THE ENGINE ROOM

10 CANE RUM

PROJECT: 10 Cane Rum DESIGN FIRM: Werner Design Werks, Inc. CLIENT: Moët Hennessy DESIGNERS: Sharon Werner, Sarah Nelson ART DIRECTOR: Sharon Werner ILLUSTRATOR: Elvis Swift FONTS USED: Minion, ITC Franklin Gothic, Trade Gothic Extended, custom

TRINIDAD, KINGDOM OF RUM

RUM

10 CANE RUM

SACCHARUM OFFICINARUM

40% ALC/VOL

1 LITER

DISTILLING PERFECTION
FROM FIRST PRESS
CANE

IMPORTED

"10 Cane is a luxury rum made for mixing top-quality rum cocktails. Alchemy was the underlying positioning of both the product and the package. The mixing of the elegant and classic crest with the irreverent placement of the label, the combination of the raw beauty of Trinidad and the sophistication of France—these are important to developing the alchemy of the brand. The simple custom bottle is designed to be bartender-friendly: easy to grip and easy to pour. 10 Cane is a new classic."

—WERNER DESIGN WERKS, INC.

"We developed a visual language and style that naturally embodies the history, elegance and eclecticism of the market, the neighborhood and New Yorkers."

—MUCCA DESIGN

BUTTERFIELD MARKET

PROJECT: Butterfield Market **DESIGN FIRM:** Mucca Design **CLIENT:** Butterfield Market **DESIGNERS:** Christine Celic Strohl, Lauren Sheldon **ART DIRECTOR:** Matteo Bologna **FONTS USED:** Bureau Grotesque, Adobe Jenson, Burin Sans, Rockwell, Zeppelin, Monoline Script, custom

DAUB & BAUBLE

PROJECT: Daub & Bauble **DESIGN FIRM:** Wink, Incorporated **CLIENT:**
Daub & Bauble **DESIGNER:** Richard Boynton **ART DIRECTORS:** Richard Boynton,
Scott Thares **FONTS USED:** New Century Schoolbook, Trade Gothic Extended

"Countertop soaps and lotions have become more home décor accessories than just cleaning products: an expression of the consumer's interior design sensibility. D&B's edition packaging is comprised of three patterns for each fragrance (modern, classic and toile), all of which are refreshed with every reprint, allowing consumers to continually update their aesthetic, just like the strategically placed coffee table book or the newly acquired throw pillow."

—WINK, INCORPORATED

HARRODS OPULENCE |||

PROJECT: Harrods Opulence DESIGN FIRM: Honey Creative CLIENT: Sarah
Paskell DESIGNER: Greg Schultz ART DIRECTOR: Doug James FONTS USED:
Snell Roundhand, ITC Cheltenham, Gill Sans

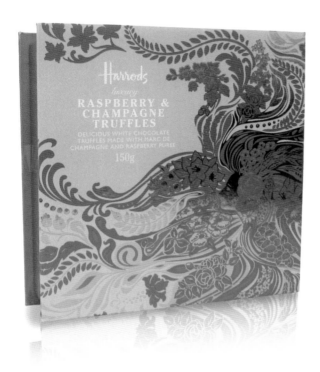

"Honey was asked to create a new sub-brand for the Harrods range in order to
fulfill the demand for a wider, more contemporary selection of premium confectionary goods. The award-winning Opulence range was inspired by the goddess
Fortuna, an icon who has reflected the decadence and luxury of Harrods since
1909. The main challenge we faced was managing the quality control for the gold
foil embossing from printers globally, due to the lack of a standard Pantone reference for foils."

—HONEY CREATIVE

PROJECT: JAQK Cellars DESIGN FIRM: Hatch Design CLIENT: JAQK Cellars
DESIGNERS: Ryan Meis, Eszter Clark, Katie Jain, Joel Templin
ART DIRECTORS: Katie Jain, Joel Templin COPYWRITER: Vinnie Chieco

JAQK CELLARS

"JAQK is the first hatchling from a partnership between Hatch Design and Craig MacLean, one of Napa Valley's most acclaimed winemakers. Named after the jack, ace, queen and king in the deck of cards, JAQK Cellars is the playful brand name for eight distinctive limited-production wines, all released in October 2008."

—HATCH DESIGN

"For High Roller, we designed a custom glass bottle. The JAQK name and decorative elements are embossed, and the bottle includes a flat surface that holds a standard poker chip perfectly. Each poker chip is then screen printed with the vintage of the wine and applied by hand to the bottle. Black Clover has a club pattern screen printed over the entire bottle surface, then a paper label applied over that. Soldiers of Fortune is designed to look like an old playing card is applied to the bottle. The Pearl Handle labels were printed with a combination of five inks on the front label, then a spot varnish, followed by turning over the label stock and printing the back sides with either a red or black spot color, depending on the suit. 22 Black, Bone Dance, Her Majesty and Charmed are screen printed directly on the glass, which allowed us to take advantage of the entire surface area."

—HATCH DESIGN

JAQK CELLARS

PROJECT: JAQK Cellars DESIGN FIRM: Hatch Design CLIENT: JAQK Cellars
DESIGNERS: Ryan Meis, Eszter Clark, Katie Jain, Joel Templin
ART DIRECTORS: Katie Jain, Joel Templin COPYWRITER: Vinnie Chieco

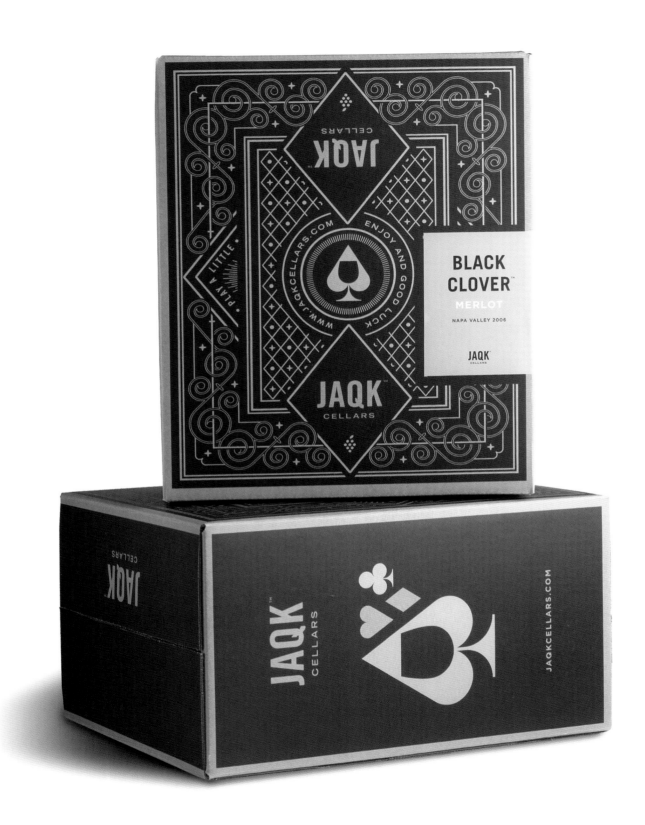

"The JAQK Gift Box makes a beautiful and protective home to our wines. Customers can choose any combination of four wines to include in the gift box and they always come complete with a deck of custom JAQK Premier Edition playing cards. We illustrated the entire deck of cards, had them printed with metallic inks by the U.S. Playing Card Company, and housed them in a charcoal, foil-stamped package."

—HATCH DESIGN

MOLTON BROWN

PROJECT: Molton Brown 2008 gift boxes DESIGN FIRM: Jones Knowles Ritchie CLIENT: Molton Brown DESIGNER: Della Lawrence ART DIRECTOR: John Ewles FONTS USED: Interstate Regular, Interstate Light

"Every year, we try to create a new look for the Christmas boxes that is beautiful enough to put under the tree without wrapping. This year, we created a confident look by using the Molton Brown type as a graphic pattern and incorporating some of the traditional elements of gift wrapping."

—JONES KNOWLES RITCHIE

12 BRIDGES GIN

PROJECT: 12 Bridges Gin **DESIGN FIRM:** ID Branding **CLIENT:** Integrity Spirits **DESIGNER:** Egon Selby **ART DIRECTOR:** Jared Milam **COPYWRITER:** Charla Adams **FONTS USED:** custom

"When our client, Integrity Spirits, wanted to make a gin that shook up the gin world, we were asked to come up with a brand that embodied their aspirations. Since Portland, Oregon, is the home of Integrity Spirits, and since their gin uses twelve botanicals for its distinct flavor, we suggested calling it 12 Bridges Gin, in honor of the twelve bridges that cross Portland's two rivers. Each bottle batch is printed with the story of a different bridge, until, over the next several years, all twelve of Portland's bridges have had their story told."

—ID BRANDING

"Root: 1 tells the story of the original ungrafted Cabernet Sauvignon rootstock, extinct in Europe and now found only in Chile. The rich history of the rootstock is visually linked to the final glass of wine, an image of which is hidden in the vine. As you read the story, the root leads you down to where it all begins, beneath the soil. A gardener's tab creates a unique neck label and emphasizes the horticultural theme."

—TURNER DUCKWORTH

PROJECT: Root: 1 DESIGN FIRM: Turner Duckworth (London & San Francisco) CLIENT: Click Wine Group CREATIVE DIRECTORS: David Turner, Bruce Duckworth DESIGNER: Shawn Rosenberger ILLUSTRATOR: Shawn Rosenberger COPYWRITER: David Turner FONT USED: Mrs Eaves

ROOT: 1

SOFIA MINI

PROJECT: Sofia mini packaging **DESIGN FIRM:** In-house art department **CLIENT:** Francis Ford Coppola Presents, LLC **DESIGNER:** Gundolf Pfotenhauer **ART DIRECTOR:** Gundolf Pfotenhauer

"The idea was to create an alternative package for a single-serve sparkling wine. Looking at a wide range of products, the aluminum can became the most desirable, fun and flexible choice. It was never done before, so it was no surprise that we had to overcome many barriers before it was ready to go into the market."

—FRANCIS COPPOLA

"Freshly cut tulips from a florist's shop were our inspiration for this promotional spring home fragrance. We transformed a plain perfume bottle with a spray pump into a tulip in a vase on a shoestring budget using straws and carefully folded, origami-inspired paper."

—ATELIER DU PRESSE-CITRON

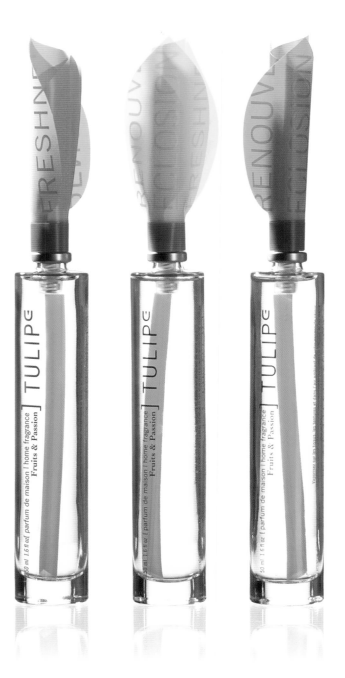

FRUITS & PASSION TULIP(E)

PROJECT: TULIP(e) **DESIGN FIRM**: Atelier du Presse-Citron **CLIENT**: Fruits & Passion **DESIGNERS**: Suzanne Côté, Jocelyn Laplante **ART DIRECTORS**: Suzanne Côté, Jocelyn Laplante **COPYWRITER**: Pascal Henrard **FONT USED**: Trade Gothic

LE TOURMENT VERT

PROJECT: Le Tourment Vert DESIGN FIRM: Turner Duckworth (London & San Francisco) CLIENT: Distillerie Vinet Ege DESIGNER DIRECTOR: Sarah Moffat DESIGNERS: Rebecca Williams, Britt Hull ILLUSTRATORS: John Geary, Christopher Garvey

"This authentic absinthe was created by Vinet Ege distillery in France for limited distribution. Our design was inspired by the swirling, cloudy patterns that form when absinthe is mixed with water."

—PEARLFISHER

"Absinthe has a controversial history, and its effects have been the subject of heated debate. It has long been a source of inspiration for artists, but its potency is not to be taken lightly ('Le Tourment Vert' means literally 'The Green Curse'). The images that appear in the swirls express this almost mystical quality. The bottle shape was inspired by the water carafes found in cafés throughout France. The secondary labels that carry legally required information were deliberately left undesigned to adapt to differing regulatory requirements governing the sale of absinthe around the world, and they can be easily removed."

—PEARLFISHER

VERY CHIC WINES

PROJECT: Very Chic **DESIGN FIRM:** So Chic Wines **CLIENT:** So Chic Wines
DESIGNERS: Laurent Pamato, Florian Battestini **ART DIRECTOR:** Laurent
Pamato **PHOTOGRAPHER:** Laurent Pamato **COPYWRITER:** Florian Battestini

"Our wines aim at a trendy urban audience concerned with fashion, luxury and quality. Very Chic will appeal to connoisseurs, as well as amateurs, looking for novelty and surprises. Each wine-tasting session is a unique moment that subtly unveils the know-how and the passion of our art.

As fashion designers would do, our winegrowers accurately and patiently designed their wines. From grape gathering to wine bottling, everything is hand-made so as to respect the noble material."

—SO CHIC WINES

"Our client wanted the branding to be sophisticated and to convey the exotic spirit of colonial Indochina, where the liqueur is said to have originated. Since the bottle already had an Asian look reminiscent of bamboo, we designed the label with an overtly turn-of-the-century French sensibility and type style."

—MUCCA DESIGN

DOMAINE DE CANTON

PROJECT: Domaine de Canton DESIGN FIRM: Mucca Design

CLIENT: Domaine de Canton DESIGNERS: Andrea Brown, Ariana DiLibero

ART DIRECTOR: Andrea Brown CREATIVE DIRECTOR: Matteo Bologna

FONTS USED: Argent Font Family

COCO MONOI

PROJECT: Coco Monoi DESIGN FIRM: Duffy & Partners CLIENT: Thymes
DESIGNERS: Ken Sakurai, Allison Newhouse ART DIRECTOR: Dan Olson
COPYWRITER: Lisa Pemrick

"We tried to create sophistication through interweaving materials, surprising colors and expressive art elements. An overflow of flower and leaf art (inspired by one of the main fragrant essences, gardenia) was juxtaposed against the subtle color transitions to create a needed upscale value. During the bottle production, we were reminded how a subtle color shift changes the feel of design dramatically."

—DUFFY & PARTNERS

"The challenge was to create an irreverent brand personality that complements Kilo Kai's premium quality and authenticity. In a category rife with visual clichés, we added a touch of wit and style to one of the biggest clichés—the skull-and-crossbones symbol—by crafting two *K*s to form the skull's teeth and bones.

Kilo Kai gets the benefit of the symbol's built-in messaging along with a fresh, ownable look that energizes the moribund rum category. The bottle's matte finish adds to the premium feel, and bottlenecks wrapped in grip tape provide tactile touch memory for bartenders."

—TURNER DUCKWORTH

PROJECT: Kilo Kai DESIGN FIRM: Turner Duckworth (London & San Francisco) CLIENT: Apostrophe Brands CREATIVE DIRECTORS: David Turner, Bruce Duckworth DESIGN DIRECTOR: Shawn Rosenberger DESIGNERS: David Turner, Tanawat Pisanuwongse FONTS USED: Copperplate Gothic, Hoefler Text, Univers

KILO KAI

TCHO CHOCOLATE

PROJECT: TCHO packaging system DESIGN FIRM: Edenspiekermann CLIENT: TCHO Ventures Inc. DESIGNERS: Susanna Dulkinys, Tobias Trost ART DIRECTOR: Susanna Dulkinys COPYWRITER: Louis Rossetto FONT USED: FF Unit

"TCHO is the first high-profile chocolate manufacturer to be established in the Bay Area since the incorporation of the Ghirardelli Company in 1852. Thus, TCHO represents an ambitious beginning that can be viewed in a significant historical context. In their product development, the founders identified six dominant natural aromas in the chocolate flavor spectrum: chocolatey, earthy, nutty, fruity, floral and citrusy. It is these distinct flavors on which the product line formulation is based."

—TCHO VENTURES INC.

GOLDEN STAR TEA

PROJECT: Golden Star Tea Company packaging and bottle design **DESIGN FIRM:** Elixir Design, Inc. **CLIENT:** Golden Star Tea Company **DESIGNERS:** Aine Coughlan, Syd Buffman **ART DIRECTOR:** Jennifer Jerde **PHOTOGRAPHER:** David Lüttschwager **COPYWRITER:** Golden Star Tea Company **FONTS USED:** Custom, Trade Gothic, Gotham, Sackers Gothic

"Golden Star Tea Company approached Elixir with an innovative product vision that would redefine how nonalcoholic beverages and teas are perceived and experienced by high-end consumers. The team at Golden Star had taken years to develop the first-ever sparkling floral tea, tasting and testing many teas and refining their fermentation process. The result is an organic infusion that mimics the mouthfeel of champagne—without the alcohol. Through the packaging design, Elixir helped to blend tea's rich history with sophisticated positioning as an ultra-premium alternative to fine still and sparkling wines."

—ELIXIR DESIGN, INC.

RED CHERIE

PROJECT: Red Cherie **DESIGN FIRM:** Duffy & Partners **CLIENT:** Thymes
DESIGNER: Candice Leick **ART DIRECTOR:** Dan Olson **COPYWRITER:** Lisa Pemrick

"The goal of this collection was to design a package that reflected the natural ingredients and exotic fruits appealing to a health-conscious consumer. Happy and sophisticated with a sense of movement were the characteristics that inspired the hand-painted art and its placement on each product and package in the collection."

—DUFFY & PARTNERS

COWSHED

PROJECT: Cowshed **DESIGN FIRM:** Pearlfisher **CLIENT:** Soho House group
DESIGNER: Karen Welman **FONT USED:** Arial

"Inspired by the interiors of Babington House, where the original Cowshed spa is located, our designs use wallpaper patterns of differing colors and textures to echo the benefit and main ingredient of each product. A touch of warmth is added through the understated copy, which creates a more subtle version of Cowshed's unique sense of humor. The result is a beautifully unbranded brand that brings the casual elegance of Babington to a bathroom."

—PEARLFISHER

EMPORIUM COLLECTION

PROJECT: Emporium collection **DESIGN FIRM:** MOR Cosmetics
DESIGNERS: Dianna Burmas, Deon St. Mor **COPYWRITER:** Danielle Flores

"The Emporium range was created to replace and
expand upon an existing range called the Soap Gallery.
We found that we did quite well with soaps, but
we were most known for our luxurious packaging.
We wanted to create a giftable luxury item that would
become a calling card for MOR."

—MOR COSMETICS

HALVORS

PROJECT: Halvors DESIGN FIRM: Tank Design CLIENT: Halvors
Tradisjonsfisk DESIGNER: Sandro Kvernmo ART DIRECTOR: Bjørn Viggo
Ottem PHOTOGRAPHERS: Helge A. Wold [Museum of Tromsø], Jean Gaumy
[Norwegian Seafood Export Council] COPYWRITER: Kari Gjæver Pedersen
FONTS USED: Neutraface, Farnham

> "Using only cheap, uncoated cardboard and one color, the aim was to show the honest and traditional approach of the product. This helps the product differentiate itself on store shelves."

—TANK DESIGN

"Office helped launch Korbin Kameron's limited-production wines by developing the brand's visual identity. The logo was created as a modern interpretation of vine tendrils; their free-form yet geometric nature reflects the art and science aspects of wine making. The simplicity of the packaging sets the brand apart from more traditional approaches to wine labeling, providing a sense of modern elegance and sophistication."

—OFFICE: JASON SCHULTE DESIGN, INC.

KORBIN KAMERON

PROJECT: Korbin Kameron identity and packaging **DESIGN FIRM:** Office: Jason Schulte Design, Inc. **CLIENT:** Korbin Kameron **DESIGNER:** Jason Schulte **CREATIVE DIRECTOR:** Jason Schulte **FONTS USED:** Trade Gothic, Filosofia

THYMES NAIA

PROJECT: Thymes Naia DESIGN FIRM: Zeus Jones CLIENT: Thymes DESIGNER: Brad Surcey ART DIRECTOR: Brad Surcey PHOTOGRAPHER: Tom Matre FONTS USED: Custom, Bryant

"Naia, the latest bath and body collection from Thymes, is a clean, crisp fragrance that activates the senses. The packaging highlights the fresh simplicity of the products by wrapping them in illustrations of translucent leaves and splashes of water."

—ZEUS JONES

BOTTICELLI ILLUMINATED CHOCOLATES

PROJECT: Botticelli Illuminated Chocolates **DESIGN FIRM:** Struck
CLIENT: Dynamic Confections **DESIGNER:** Dan Christofferson **ART DIRECTOR:**
Peter Singleton **COPYWRITER:** Rich Black **FONTS USED:** Rockwell,
Akzidenz-Grotesk, Berthold City

"Fighting to bridge the gap between commodity and luxury, Botticelli enlisted
us to craft a visual brand and package design that reflect and exceed the current
demand for premium confectionary chocolates. Looking directly to the Italian
artist Botticelli for inspiration, we recalled Botticelli's apprenticeship as a gold-
smith to develop a packaging system that mimics the shape of a gold bar, the
name, the descriptor 'illuminated chocolates,' the nods to Renaissance artwork—
all to provide a well-rounded tribute to Botticelli's legacy."

—STRUCK

SOLERNO

PROJECT: Solerno **DESIGN FIRM:** Stranger & Stranger **CLIENT:** William Grant & Sons **DESIGNERS:** Kevin Shaw, Guy Pratt **ART DIRECTOR:** Kevin Shaw **PHOTOGRAPHER:** Karin Taylor **FONTS USED:** Didot, Burgues Script

"The orange liqueur market is dominated by two old French brands. Solerno was developed as a modern and lighter alternative, and it was aimed firmly at the *Sex and the City* female market. The bottle is inspired by the famous Italian glassmakers in Murano, and the punt is designed around a classic orange juice squeezer. It took more than two years to get into production because of the intricacy of the base."

—STRANGER & STRANGER

CHAPTER 2
BOLD

BOLD: BRIGHT, COLORFUL, EYE-CATCHING,
UNAFRAID, ADVENTUROUS, FEARLESS.
THIS SECTION IS ALL ABOUT PACKAGING THAT
STANDS OUT AND ISN'T AFRAID TO MAKE
A STATEMENT.

AZITA'S HOT SAUCE

PROJECT: Azita's Almost-All-American Hot Sauce DESIGN FIRM:
Verse Creative CLIENT: Azita's DESIGNER: Michael Freimuth
ART DIRECTOR: Michael Freimuth COPYWRITER: Michael Freimuth
FONTS USED: Fairplex, HTF Knockout, House Script

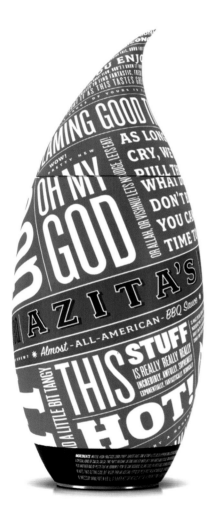

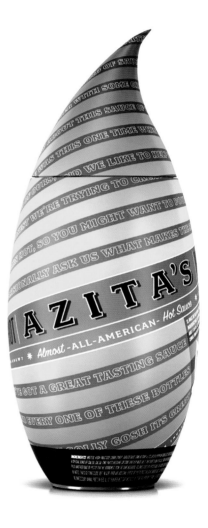

"Azita's Almost-All-American Hot Sauce is really a product of the woman behind
the brand. As the owner and Persian chef of a start-up cookshop in Chicago, Azita
continues to be an incredibly energetic and charismatic client and personality. We
attempted to draw from that character to inform the diversely expressive design."

—VERSE CREATIVE

"A ready-to-drink cocktail, G&T uses an X and an O to cut through the clutter of busy alcohol packaging. The caps become tic-tac-toe pieces and encourage consumers to interact with the brand after consumption."

—DIANA LUISTRO

G&T

PROJECT: G&T DESIGNER: Diana Luistro CLIENT: None (student project)
ART DIRECTOR: Diana Luistro PHOTOGRAPHER: Diana Luistro COPYWRITER: Diana Luistro FONTS USED: Helvetica Neue (bold and regular)

BEAUTAO ACTIVE BOTANICALS

PROJECT: Beautao Active Botanicals **DESIGN FIRM**: Miller Creative LLC **CLIENT**: Dermapeutics Corporation **DESIGNER**: Yael Miller **PHOTOGRAPHER**: Andre Jackametz **COPYWRITER**: Taqiyyah Shakirah Dawud **FONT USED**: Helvetica Neue

"This project included brand naming, logo and packaging design. The budget for the project did not allow for any embossing or specialized coatings in the end, but the careful selection of custom Pantone spot colors enable this collection to really stand out."

—MILLER CREATIVE

ACTIVATE

PROJECT: Activate packaging **DESIGN FIRM:** LeeReedy **CLIENT:** Activate
DESIGNERS: Ben Peiratt, Patrick Gill **ART DIRECTORS:** Kelly Reedy, Patrick Gill **PHOTOGRAPHER:** Mark Laita **COPYWRITERS:** Jamie Reedy, Eric Kiker
FONTS USED: Futura, Synchro LET

"The biggest challenge was creating a label and package that showcased the product's activation while communicating that there were multiple flavors. The use of color gradients starting strong and evaporating to nothing solved it. The drop icons were just candy."

—LEEREEDY

"The brief was to create an innovation in the category, challenging the traditional beer aesthetics. The sales have proven that this has become a success among consumers."

—TANK DESIGN

PROJECT: Smrprty DESIGN FIRM: Tank Design CLIENT: Mack Brewery
DESIGNERS: Bernt Ottem, Bjørn Viggo Ottem FONT USED: Helvetica

SMRPRTY

PUBLIC MARKET

PROJECT: Public Market on Granville Island reusable bags **DESIGN FIRM:** Saint Bernadine Mission Communications Inc. **CLIENT:** CMHC Granville Island **DESIGNERS:** Sofia Roberts, Megan Seely **ART DIRECTORS:** Andrew Samuel, Sofia Roberts **COPYWRITERS:** David Walker, Robyn Smith

"We wanted to create a reusable shopping bag that was actually attractive, while still being durable and usable. In addition, we wanted the design to reflect the vibrancy that the Public Market on Granville Island is known for."

—SAINT BERNADINE MISSION COMMUNICATIONS INC.

UGLY MUG COFFEE

PROJECT: Ugly Mug Coffee packaging redesign **DESIGN FIRM:** Young & Laramore Advertising **CLIENT:** Ugly Mug Coffee Co. **DESIGNER:** Yee-Haw Industries **ART DIRECTOR:** Trevor Williams **PHOTOGRAPHER:** Harold Lee Miller **COPYWRITER:** Bryan Judkins **FONTS USED:** None (letterpress: lead and wood type)

"The design approach is analogous to how the company approaches coffee: with enough seriousness to compete with other high-end specialty coffees, and with the irreverence and good humor implied by the Ugly Mug Coffee name. We used traditional letterpress to create a signature graphic tone, largely because letterpress is both unpretentious and painstakingly handcrafted—ugly and beautiful."

—YOUNG & LARAMORE ADVERTISING

UGLY MUG COFFEE

SAVING GRACE

BALANCED

HIGH TONES • CLEAN FINISH
NOT TOO LIGHT • BUT WET, NOT TOO DARK

WHOLE BEAN COFFEE

GUATEMALA / PERU

WE AIN'T GOT NO ALIBI

THIS COFFEE...

HAILS FROM MEMPHIS. THE SEATTLE OF SOUTHWESTERN TENNESSEE • IS PURCHASED, ROASTED AND PACKAGED WITH A LITTLE SOMETHING WE LIKE TO CALL INTEGRITY • REMINDS US OF A TIME BEFORE THE DOUBLE MINT MOCHA DECAF SKIM LATTE RULED THE EARTH • KNOWS GOOD LOOKS WILL ONLY GET YOU SO FAR • SPEAKS WITHOUT RESORTING TO FAUX EUROPEAN WORDS, EXCEPT FAUX • UNDERSTANDS YOU, MAYBE TOO WELL • WORKS BEST WITH ONE OR TWO TABLESPOONS OF GROUND COFFEE PER 6 OUNCES OF WATER • IS THE LATEST BUNDLE OF JOY FROM UGLY MUG COFFEE.

UGLY MUG COFFEE CO.

UGLY MUG COFFEE

HARDY PASSION

BOLD

ROBUST • RICH • ALL DARK AND NO BITE

WHOLE BEAN COFFEE

MEXICO / PERU

YOU ARE NOW LEAVING SLEEPY-TOWN

THIS COFFEE...

HAILS FROM MEMPHIS. THE SEATTLE OF SOUTHWESTERN TENNESSEE • IS PURCHASED, ROASTED AND PACKAGED WITH A LITTLE SOMETHING WE LIKE TO CALL INTEGRITY • REMINDS US OF A TIME BEFORE THE DOUBLE MINT MOCHA DECAF SKIM LATTE RULED THE EARTH • KNOWS GOOD LOOKS WILL ONLY GET YOU SO FAR • SPEAKS WITHOUT RESORTING TO FAUX EUROPEAN WORDS, EXCEPT FAUX • UNDERSTANDS YOU, MAYBE TOO WELL • WORKS BEST WITH ONE OR TWO TABLESPOONS OF GROUND COFFEE PER 6 OUNCES OF WATER • IS THE LATEST BUNDLE OF JOY FROM UGLY MUG COFFEE.

UGLY MUG COFFEE CO.

UGLY MUG COFFEE

GOOD VIBES

BALANCED

EVEN • FULL-BODIED • SWEET AROMA
AN EMBARRASSMENT OF RICH

WHOLE BEAN COFFEE

ORGANICALLY GROWN / FAIR TRADE

WAKE The WAKE OF THE JUST

THIS COFFEE...

HAILS FROM MEMPHIS. THE SEATTLE OF SOUTHWESTERN TENNESSEE • IS PURCHASED, ROASTED AND PACKAGED WITH A LITTLE SOMETHING WE LIKE TO CALL INTEGRITY • REMINDS US OF A TIME BEFORE THE DOUBLE MINT MOCHA DECAF SKIM LATTE RULED THE EARTH • KNOWS GOOD LOOKS WILL ONLY GET YOU SO FAR • SPEAKS WITHOUT RESORTING TO FAUX EUROPEAN WORDS, EXCEPT FAUX • UNDERSTANDS YOU, MAYBE TOO WELL • WORKS BEST WITH ONE OR TWO TABLESPOONS OF GROUND COFFEE PER 6 OUNCES OF WATER • IS THE LATEST BUNDLE OF JOY FROM UGLY MUG COFFEE.

UGLY MUG COFFEE CO.

CHOCOLATE RESEARCH FACILITY

PROJECT: Chocolate Research Facility DESIGN FIRM: Asylum CLIENT: Chocolate Research Facility DESIGNER: Yong ART DIRECTORS: Cara Ang, Chris Lee PHOTOGRAPHER: Lumina FONTS USED: Memphis, Rockwell Extra Bold

"The goal was to design 100 flavors that have a uniform look and yet are different and exciting. We managed to cluster them in series with different graphic elements."

—ASYLUM

BASIC

PROJECT: Basic DESIGN FIRM: Enric Aguilera Asociados CLIENT:
La Sirena DESIGNER: Marius Zorrilla ART DIRECTOR: Enric Aguilera
FONT USED: Trade Gothic

"La Sirena wanted to differentiate its products and to create a line that's low cost.
The goal was a simpler image."

—ENRIC AGUILERA ASOCIADOS

"Miller Chill was the opportunity to create a category. We were developing a new alternative to premium beers that captured the imagination of consumers by combining the intrigue of an import with the refreshing 'drinkability' of a light domestic."

—OPTIMA SOULSIGHT

PROJECT: Miller Chill DESIGN FIRM: Optima Soulsight CLIENT: Miller Brewing Company DESIGNERS: Adam Ferguson, Jim Pietruszynski, Aaron Funke ART DIRECTOR: Lyle Zimmerman FONTS USED: Handlettering, Bickham Script

MILLER CHILL

PROJECT: DOO Smoothie **DESIGN FIRM:** B&T Design **CLIENT:** DOO
DESIGNERS: Yohan Baillet, Julien Thebault **ART DIRECTORS' NAMES:**
Yohan Baillet, Julien Thebault

DOO

"We chose the name DOO because it reminds us of the word 'sweet' in French—
in a nicer way. DOO's market is exclusively in France, and we wanted to stand out
from the other products with a strong and fresh identity."

—B&T DESIGN

YOSHI-GO

PROJECT: Yoshi-Go **DESIGN FIRM:** LA+B, Love for Art & Business **CLIENT:** Haruna Ecology Japan, Haruna Europe **ART DIRECTOR:** Sarah Sheppard **DESIGNER:** Sarah Sheppard **CREATIVE DIRECTOR:** Jonas Lundin **PHOTOGRAPHER:** LA+B **COPYWRITERS:** Emi Gunér, Louise Hunter **FONTS USED:** Modified Futura, custom Japanese fonts

"This project started with one simple brief: Create a new consumer product from our high-grade green tea. We were involved in everything, including product development, naming, insights with focus groups, fine-tuning of recipes, marketing strategies and design. It was very hard work spanning over two years' time. The biggest reward for us was to see it become a success in so many markets worldwide."

—LA+B

"We designed and created a brand universe with two key elements: the main ingredient (olive oil) and the location of use (the kitchen). The brand combines a strong name and a friendly, unifying, Mediterranean design. Objects that blend form and function give an effect of surprise in a familiar environment."

—ORANGETANGO

JONES GABA

PROJECT: Jones GABA **DESIGN FIRM:** Superbig Creative **CLIENT:** Jones Soda Co. **DESIGNER:** Rich Williams **ART DIRECTOR:** Kevin Walsh **COPYWRITER:** Kevin Walsh **FONTS USED:** Regular, custom

"The consistent challenges of this project were providing the client with a stimulating solution accompanied by a substantial amount of shelf appeal, and utilizing the sizable amount of information on a small surface area."

—SUPERBIG CREATIVE

"Waitrose Herbs have a lot to say for themselves. Each minimally packaged bunch of herbs carries bold, tabloid-style text, telling you all you may or may not know about the contents. Guest herbs make an exclusive and seasonal appearance with a splash of red in the headline."

—LEWIS MOBERLY

Waitrose COOKS' INGREDIENTS

THE BEAUTIFUL BAY LEAF
SAVOURY OR SWEET
COMFORTING IN CUSTARDS, SUBTLE IN STEWS
INFUSE YOUR OILS AND PEP UP YOUR PIES
THE ESSENTIAL BOUQUET GARNI OR 'BACCALAUREATE'
GARLANDS OF BAY TO HONOUR THE SCHOLAR

Waitrose COOKS' INGREDIENTS

COOL COOL MINT
NOT JUST FOR JELLY!
INFUSE YOUR TEA, DRESS UP YOUR DRINKS
PAIR UP WITH PEAS OR SUMMER SORBET

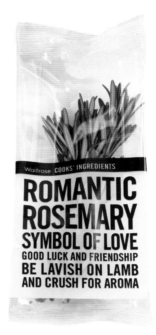

Waitrose COOKS' INGREDIENTS

ROMANTIC ROSEMARY
SYMBOL OF LOVE
GOOD LUCK AND FRIENDSHIP
BE LAVISH ON LAMB AND CRUSH FOR AROMA

Waitrose COOKS' INGREDIENTS

MAJESTIC BASIL
'KING OF THE HERBS'
ONCE REGARDED SACRED TO THE GODS
FRAGRANT BASIL STILL REIGNS SUPREME

Waitrose COOKS' INGREDIENTS

TANTALISING TARRAGON 'FINE HERBS'
FAVOURED IN FRANCE FAMOUS FOR TARTARE MUSTARD AND VINEGAR

Waitrose COOKS' INGREDIENTS

BORAGE HERB OF THE WEEK
SOMETHING SEASONAL OR SIMPLY SPECIAL

PROJECT: Waitrose Herbs DESIGN FIRM: Lewis Moberly CLIENT: Waitrose Ltd DESIGNER: Poppy Stedman ART DIRECTOR: Mary Lewis COPYWRITER: Mary Lewis FONT USED: Robin Gothic Bold

WAITROSE HERBS

CHAPTER 3
CRISP

CRISP: CLEAN, CONTEMPORARY, GEOMETRIC, SIMPLE, SLEEK, STYLISH, TIDY. THIS SECTION IS ALL ABOUT PACKAGING THAT REALLY LIVES UP TO THE OLD ADAGE "LESS IS MORE."

WAITROSE HONEY

PROJECT: Honey Bee **DESIGN FIRM:** Turner Duckworth (London &
San Francisco) **CLIENT:** Waitrose Ltd **CREATIVE DIRECTORS:** David Turner,
Bruce Duckworth **DESIGNER:** Christian Eager **ILLUSTRATOR:** John Geary
ARTWORKER: Reuben James **FONT USED:** Geometric BT

"Waitrose approached Turner Duckworth to redesign their entire honey range,
to make the fixture easy to navigate and bring it in line with their 'good, better,
best' tiering structure. The tiers help differentiate between 'everyday' honey for
spreading on toast, and the more specialist taste—or provenance-based honeys
that are ideal for cooking, or for that special weekend treat.

A simple typographic design, playing with the E in 'honey,' creates the
stripy body of a bee, and also references wooden honey twizzler sticks. It's a simple
design that runs across all the set and clear honeys in their 'good' tier."

—TURNER DUCKWORTH

Y WATER

PROJECT: Y Water DESIGN FIRM: fuseproject CLIENT: Y Water DESIGNERS:
Yves Behar, Josh Morenstein, Bret Recor, Nick Cronan ART DIRECTOR:
Yves Behar PHOTOGRAPHER: fuseproject FONT USED: Helvetica Rounded

"In designing the new Y Water, our intent was to create a natural and organic
beverage for kids. As an alternative to juices and sodas with high sugar content,
Y Water is a naturally flavored, USDA-certified organic beverage. Y Water also
focuses on reuse, allowing children to enjoy an organic beverage and reuse the
bottle in a fun game after consumption."

—FUSEPROJECT

FLUID

PROJECT: Fluid **DESIGN FIRM:** Tank Design **CLIENT:** Mack Brewery **DESIGNERS:** Bjørn Viggo Ottem, Sandro Kvernmo, Bernt Ottem **FONT USED:** Neo Sans

"We were asked to design a beer brand and packaging for a target group who doesn't traditionally prefer beer."

—TANK DESIGN

BAXTER OF CALIFORNIA

PROJECT: Baxter of California **DESIGN FIRM:** DIGI-AKIMO **CLIENT:** Baxter of California **DESIGNER:** Chris DiGiacomo **COPYWRITER:** Baxter of California

"The new products are intended to be displayed alongside the modern-art books and design-centric products that the Baxter guy covets and will feel at home in the world's finest grooming lounges, apothecaries, spas and lifestyle boutiques."

—DIGI-AKIMO

DRY SODA

PROJECT: DRY Soda packaging DESIGN FIRM: Turnstyle CLIENT: DRY Soda DESIGNER: Steve Watson ART DIRECTOR: Steve Watson FONT USED: Helvetica Neue

"DRY Soda produces lightly sweet, all-natural, culinary sodas that, similar to fine wines, were developed to be paired with great foods. Our design solution was intentionally minimalist. We endeavored to make the bottles sophisticated, but still fresh and inviting. Monochromatic, typographic and screen-printed labels boil product information down to their essence without extraneous bells and whistles. Minimal graphics on clear bottles allow the purity of the product to show through. The owner's signature on each bottle denotes a sense of craft behind each flavor's recipe."

—TURNSTYLE

CLEANWELL

PROJECT: CleanWell **DESIGN FIRM:** PhilippeBecker **CLIENT:** CleanWell

DESIGN TEAM: Coco Qiu, Barkha Wadia, Melanie Halim **ART DIRECTOR:**

PhilippeBecker **FONTS USED:** Akzidenz-Grotesk, Stane Sans

"Consumers have relatively low expectations in the natural-cleaning category, a category that is dominated by Purell, which is mostly alcohol and toxic to kids. CleanWell is as effective as Purell, yet it's all-natural and safe for kids. The active ingredient is Ingenium, a patent formulation of botanically sourced essential plant oils that kill 99.99 percent of harmful germs. Our brand and package had to communicate efficacy while still feeling like a natural brand. To us, natural meant clean, pure and fresh. The strong brand against an uncluttered white background communicated the right balance of purity and power."

—PHILIPPEBECKER

HIGH VALE
CORE PRESERVES

PROJECT: High Vale Core Preserves **DESIGN FIRM:** brainCELLS
CLIENT: High Vale Orchard **DESIGNER:** Brett Layton **ART DIRECTOR:**
Steve Boros **FONTS USED:** DIN, Avenir

"A range of twelve biodynamic preserve labels were printed on transparent paper to show as much of the product
color as possible. The minimal label lets the product color
show so the brand speaks for itself. The preserves are all-
natural, biodynamic and organic, which is good for the
environment and good for your stomach."

—BRAINCELLS

DELISHOP BLACK LABEL

PROJECT: Delishop Black Label **DESIGN FIRM:** Enric Aguilera Asociados

CLIENT: Delishop **DESIGNER:** Gaizka Ruiz **ART DIRECTOR:** Enric Aguilera

FONT USED: Helvetica

delishop

Risotto con rúcula y espárragos
Asparagus and arugula risotto

100% natural

delishop

Aceitunas de chocolate y praliné
Chocolate and praline olives

"Black Label by Delishop is a new line of high-quality foods, following the concept of the classic line, based on the bar code."

—ENRIC AGUILERA ASOCIADOS

DOUBLE CROSS VODKA

PROJECT: Double Cross Vodka **DESIGN FIRM:** Capsule **CLIENT:** Old Nassau Imports **DESIGNERS:** Brian Adducci, Dan Baggenstoss **ART DIRECTOR:** Brian Adducci **FONTS USED:** Schindler, Indispose

"The team immersed themselves in the market, studying bottle shapes, colors, labels and all other brand-defining characteristics. The team married opulence with history, and energy with extravagance, to create a cohesive look. A Slovakian poem cascades down the back of the bottle, small touches of red add a certain depth and richness, while the clean and sleek lines scream modern luxury. With the exception of a tamperproof seal, the bottle is without labels, as all graphics are embedded within the glass. The final result is the first rectangular bottle in the vodka category that has a design that blends old with new, but also creates the starkest contrast between those two worlds. The bottle becomes the brand, and the brand becomes the bottle."

—CAPSULE

"We wanted to express the purity and clearness from up here at 70° North. (It's really not that far from the North Pole.)"

—TANK DESIGN

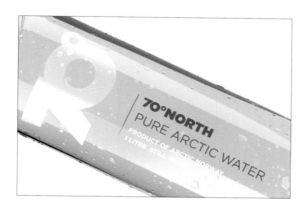

PROJECT: 70°North DESIGN FIRM: Tank Design CLIENT: Alta Water Company DESIGNERS: Jens K Styve, Bjørn Viggo Ottem, Simen Justdal, Per Finne FONT USED: Gotham

70°NORTH

BLOSSA ANNUAL EDITION

PROJECT: Blossa Annual Edition **DESIGN FIRM:** BVD **CLIENT:** V&S Group
DESIGNERS: Mia Heijkenskjöld, Sofia Ekvall **DESIGN DIRECTOR:** Susanna
Nygren Barrett **CREATIVE DIRECTOR:** Catrin Vagnemark **FONTS USED:** Didot
(2003), Futura Black (2004), Modified FatFace (2005), Dividend (2006), Umbra
(2007), illustration (2008)

"Blossa's annual edition mulled wine has been a huge
success since its launch for the 2003 Christmas season,
with an increase in popularity each year. This year,
more than 500,000 of the limited-edition bottles were
sold out in only a few weeks. It has been featured on more
than 100 international blogs and in hundreds of press
clippings, and it has received numerous design awards."

—BVD

"Lazarus Wine is outstanding for its innovative process of elaboration. In this processing, a blind enologist, with the support of a team of professionals, carried out sensorial trials. The primary objective of the trials was to achieve a wine of the highest quality, elaborated by sensorial methods. In the design of the label, the most modern techniques have been employed and inspired by the forms of the tactile Braille system. The aims of the label were to highlight the wine-making process, to make the label intelligible for the blind population and to present an outstanding wine with great appeal for the general public."

—BAUD

LAZARUS WINE

PROJECT: Lazarus Wine **DESIGN FIRM:** Baud **CLIENT:** Lazaruswine Elaboración Sensorial S.L. **DESIGNER:** Carlos Corral Madrigal **ART DIRECTOR:** Carlos Corral Madrigal **FONTS USED:** Braille Universal, Helvetica

MELT

PROJECT: Melt DESIGN FIRM: Jesse Kirsch CLIENT: None (student project)

DESIGNER: Jesse Kirsch PHOTOGRAPHER: Jesse Kirsch FONTS USED: custom

"Melt, a gourmet chocolate shop, plays with the characteristics of melted chocolate in its logo and packaging in a fun, unexpected and sophisticated way."

—JESSE KIRSCH

LIL' BOWL BLU & LE SCRUB

PROJECT: Lil' Bowl Blu and Le Scrub DESIGN FIRM: Method Products CLIENT: Method Products DESIGNERS: Danny Alexander, Josh Handy ART DIRECTOR: Stef Hermsdorf PHOTOGRAPHER: Todd Tankersley COPYWRITER: Melissa Sheehan FONT USED: Avenir

"For Lil' Bowl Blu, we designed the bottle to be just as friendly as the formula inside—cute, soft and squeezy—with the perfect angle for squirting under the rim, and with an embossed pattern to help you grip with ease. It's the first toilet bowl cleaner you might actually leave out for guests to see.

Le Scrub uses finely milled marble as a natural abrasive to gently scrub away even the toughest stains, leaving nothing behind but the sweet smell of eucalyptus and mint. The bottle has a built-in sponge holder to keep your sponge from wandering too far and getting too icky—no more rummaging under your bathroom sink."

—METHOD

APOTHIA

PROJECT NAME: Apothia Los Angeles Hand & Body Wash **DESIGN FIRM:** Through Smoke Creative **CLIENT:** Ron Robinson **DESIGNER:** Matthew Fadness **ART DIRECTOR:** Gary McNatton **PHOTOGRAPHER:** Ming-Shiun Wu **COPYWRITER:** Lisa Wilson **FONTS USED:** Neutra, News Gothic

"This liquid soap collection is a functional, systematic and expressive addition to a modern kitchen or bath. The silicone band provides a nonslip grip in the shower or bath. Eight perfume-grade fragrances interpret the Los Angeles life-style through a range of scent and color. A clean, contemporary design enhances a modern home."

—RON ROBINSON

RGX

PROJECT: Right Guard RGX body spray **DESIGN FIRM:** Wallace Church, Inc.
CLIENT: The Dial Corporation **DESIGNER:** Akira Yasuda **ART DIRECTOR:**
John Bruno **DESIGN DIRECTOR:** Stan Church **FONTS USED:** KamaroArt, Bank
Gothic, Akzidenz-Grotesk BQ

"The titanium skin, compelling brand mark and vibrant yet controlled accent
colors convey a lighter-smelling lineup, contrasting the heavy-scent alternatives.
The RGX monogram and the X icon speak to the confident, contemporary male.
When combined with a twenty-first-century structure, the resulting identity is
sleek, powerful and remarkably refined."

—WALLACE CHURCH, INC.

"Our aluminum bottle design embodies Coke's renewed focus on its core brand identity. The classic contour bottle shape features an oversized Coke trademark and nothing more. This clean and confident design simplifies what it means to be Coke and makes the brand feel fresh and new again."

—TURNER DUCKWORTH

COCA-COLA ALUMINUM BOTTLE

PROJECT: Coca-Cola Aluminum Bottle DESIGN FIRM: Turner Duckworth (London & San Francisco) CLIENT: The Coca-Cola Company CREATIVE DIRECTORS: David Turner, Bruce Duckworth DESIGNER: Chris Garvey

FONT USED: Helvetica

STORIES

PROJECT: Stories **DESIGN FIRM:** BVD **CLIENT:** Turesgruppen **DESIGNER:** Johan Andersson **DESIGN DIRECTOR:** Susanna Nygren Barrett **CREATIVE DESIGNER:** Carin Blidholm Svensson **FONT USED:** The typeface is inspired by the standard Aviso pegboard letter system used by sign makers in Sweden in the mid-twentieth century, and a rare combination of Futura and Akzindenz-Grotesk

EN SÅDAN HÄR MUGG MED KAFFE RÄDDADE MAGNUS

MAGNUS FRÅN ATT SOMNA.

EN SÅ

STO ORIE ES S

"The challenge was to create a modern café environment with old-world charm and quality from concept and name, to graphic profile and packaging. The inspiration for Stories comes from the conversation, thoughts, tales and gossip that are exchanged over a café table. The black-and-white graphics are simple and bold, but at the same time surprising and playful. Small stories are found on everything from porcelain to little packets of sugar."

—BVD

SERO²

PROJECT: Sero² **DESIGN FIRM:** Curious Design Consultants Ltd. **CLIENT:** NZ Aquaceuticals Ltd. **DESIGNER:** Natalie Dawson **ART DIRECTOR:** Nigel Kuzimski **COPYWRITER:** David Bridgman **FONTS USED:** ITC Bauhaus Std, Santana

serotonin naturally

SERO²

Softly Sparkling
Serotonic
Spring Water

"The challenge for Curious was to reflect the attributes of Sero² in the packaging design. This was achieved by creating a harmonious, understated image that attracts the consumer by its simplicity and integrity."

—CURIOUS DESIGN CONSULTANTS LTD

"Our purpose was to create a bold, rebellious and differentiated packaging in bottled water—all while being honest and transparent in its message and design."

—LISA TSE CREATIVE CONSULTING

PROJECT: Tap'dNY DESIGN FIRM: Lisa Tse Creative Consulting CLIENT: Tapped, Inc. DESIGNER: Lisa Tse ART DIRECTOR: Craig Zucker COPYWRITER: Craig Zucker FONT USED: DIN

TAP'DNY

COWSHED

PROJECT: Cowshed Skincare Line **DESIGN FIRM:** Bloom **CLIENT:** Cowshed **DESIGNERS:** Paula MacFarlane, Polly Williams **ART DIRECTOR:** Dan Cornell **FONTS USED:** Clarendon, American Typewriter

COWSHED
horny cow
seductive
body lotion
soin corporel séduction coquine

with rose absolute
and essential oils of
patchouli and cinnamon

300ml ℮
10.15fl.oz

COWSHED
knackered cow
relaxing
body lotion
soin corporel détente

with essential oils of
lavender and
eucalyptus

300ml ℮
10.15fl.oz

COWSHED
lazy cow
soothing
body lotion
soin corporel douce paresse

with essential oils of
jasmine, chamomile
and sandalwood

300ml ℮
10.15fl.oz

COWSHED
moody cow
balancing
body lotion
soin corporel rééquilibrant

with essential oils of
rose geranium, linden blossom
and frankincense

300ml ℮
10.15fl.oz

COWSHED
wild cow
invigorating
body lotion
soin corporel folie stimulante

with essential oils of
lemongrass, ginger
and rosemary

300ml ℮
10.15fl.oz

COWSHED
grumpy cow
uplifting
body lotion
soin corporel dynamisant

with essential oils of
mandarin red, petitgrain
and grapefruit

300ml ℮
10.15fl.oz

"Due to the nature of Cowshed products, which are made from organic essential oils, we wanted to develop a rural foundation for the design and overlay it with a contemporary, urban tone. This engages consumers by creating a distinctive attitude and cheeky personality."

—BLOOM

GLOJI

PROJECT: Gloji bottle design **DESIGN FIRM**: Gloji, Inc. **CLIENT**: Gloji, Inc. **DESIGNER**: Peter Kao **ART DIRECTOR**: Peter Kao **PHOTOGRAPHER**: Lucy Lu **COPYWRITER**: Lucy Lu **FONT USED**: Clearly Gothic

"The idea of the Gloji package design is based on three related elements: First, the brand name 'Gloji'; second, the main ingredient, goji berry juice; and third, the slogan, 'The juice that makes you glow.' By using a lightbulb-shaped bottle, it visually communicates the ideas of 'glowing' and 'healthy.' It also represents energy, bright ideas and something that can light up your life. This innovative shape is very ergonomic and looks great as well as fits great in your hand."

—PETER KAO

"The design for Flammable is a conceptual and chic understatement. The under-designed running block of black foiled text becomes the cement that holds the blatantly irrelevant text together."

—MARC ATLAN DESIGN

This is a "Flammable" scented candle made by Baxter of California in the United States of America.

We call it: "Jasmin Noir".

It weighs nine ounces, that is two hundred and fifty five grams, and lasts for roughly seventy hours. It is made of a soy-based wax, hand-poured in New York by our friends at Joya.

||| FLAMMABLE

PROJECT: Flammable DESIGN FIRM: Marc Atlan Design, Inc. CLIENT: Baxter of California DESIGNER: Marc Atlan

DANIELE DE WINTER

PROJECT: Daniele de Winter packaging **DESIGN FIRM:** Stuttgart State Academy of Art and Design **CLIENT:** Autrepart Nature **DESIGNERS:** Gerhardt Kellermann, Benjamin Ehrhardt **ART DIRECTOR:** Atoosa Poterachi **FONT USED:** Futura

DANIELE de WINTER
MONACO

"This project was a packaging design concept in cooperation with Autrepart Nature. We were asked to redesign the existing product range of Daniele de Winter. The de Winter brand implies scientific research, natural ingredients and a high-society luxury brand. We tried to keep the packaging of the cosmetics very clean and reduced to underline the exclusive character of the brand."

—GERHARDT KELLERMANN,
BENJAMIN EHRHARDT

DANIELE *de* WINTER
MONACO

"A simple cylinder with one degree of bevel makes the product special without obvious 'styling.' The bottom part of the product is made of glass to show the background of the scientific research and stand for honesty and the highest-quality ingredients. It's evident that this product is 100 percent natural and good for your body."

—GERHARDT KELLERMANN,
BENJAMIN EHRHARDT

LIVING PROOF

PROJECT: Living Proof **DESIGN FIRM:** Wolff Olins **CLIENT:** Living Proof
DESIGNERS: Tiziana Haug, Sung Kim **CREATIVE DIRECTOR:** Todd Simmons
PRODUCTION DIRECTORS: Beth Kovalsky, Michele Miller **PHOTOGRAPHER:**
Various **COPYWRITERS:** Mary Ellen Muckerman, Carmine Montalto **FONT**
USED: DTL Documenta

"Living Proof was created to apply advanced technology to solve the toughest beauty challenges women with frizzy hair have. Our design challenge was to create an international brand that stands apart from all other beauty brands.

As each one of Living Proof's products is unique and solution-specific, we developed a packaging system that would mimic that. The packaging forms will grow into a diverse collection of shapes and sizes as the company adds new products, but always stay rooted in the selection of materials and color palette."

—WOLFF OLINS

"When approached to rebrand a line of 100 percent natural carbonated juices, BBDK responded with a simple question: Why not call it 100% Soda? Graphically, we felt that nothing said 'pure' better than clean graphics, so rather than go with a traditional four-color label, we reduced it down to a one-color typographic solution."

—BBDK

PROJECT: 100% Soda DESIGN FIRM: BBDK, Inc. CLIENT: The Switch DESIGNER: Duane King ART DIRECTOR: Duane King COPYWRITER: Duane King FONTS USED: ITC Avant Garde, Gothic Bold, Futura Bold

100% SODA

FRESH & EASY
FLAVORED WATER

PROJECT: Fresh & Easy Flavored Water **DESIGN FIRM**: Pemberton
& Whitefoord **CLIENT**: Tesco **DESIGNER**: Barry Crombie **ART DIRECTORS**:
Simon Pemberton, Adrian Whitefoord **FONT USED**: Helvetica Neue

"The key to creating a fresh, natural flavored water that had impact on the shelf
was the illusion of fruit dropping into the water."

—PEMBERTON & WHITEFOORD

TESCO NATURALLY

PROJECT: Tesco Naturally range **DESIGN FIRM:** Pemberton & Whitefoord
CLIENT: Tesco **DESIGNER:** Wesley Anson **ART DIRECTOR:** Simon Pemberton
FONT USED: Hand

"The brief was to create a brand name and strong brand identity across various packaging formats and products within the range. We used minimal design and a controlled color palette to communicate its eco credentials."

—PEMBERTON & WHITEFOORD

"The essence of the project is creating a new brand, Flavours of Podlaskie, integrating different local producers from the Podlaskie region of Poland. The graphics and visuals reference the ornamentation style of the region. Particular groups of products are identified by distinct color codes, while the essential graphic theme is based on a typical pattern of double-warp fabrics from the Podlaskie region."

—MONIKA OSTASZEWSKA

M13 FUNCTIONAL JUICE

PROJECT: M13 Functional Juice **DESIGN FIRM:** Betterdaze Press Inc.
CLIENT: M13 Functional Juice **DESIGNER:** Mark Gainor **ART DIRECTOR:** Mark
Gainor **PHOTOGRAPHER:** André Pinces **COPYWRITER:** Neil Simonton
FONT USED: Helvetica Neue

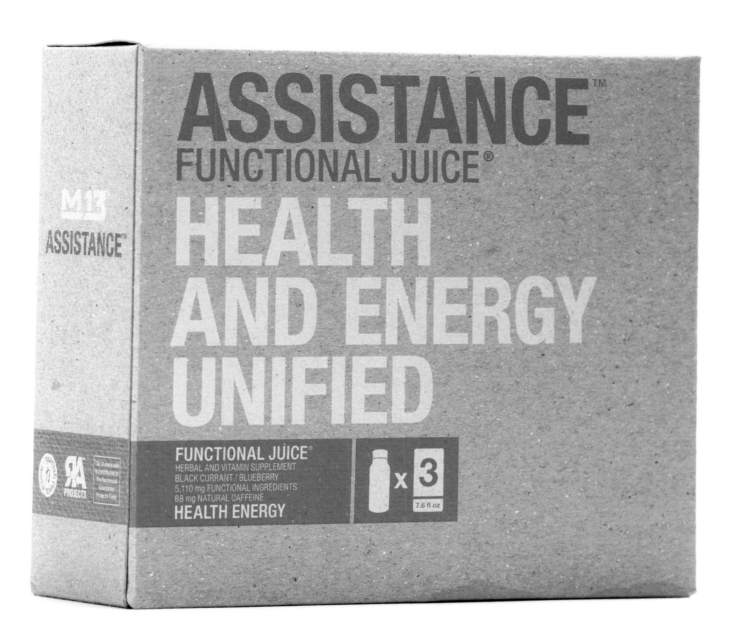

ASSISTANCE™
FUNCTIONAL JUICE®
HEALTH
AND ENERGY
UNIFIED

M13
ASSISTANCE™

FUNCTIONAL JUICE®
HERBAL AND VITAMIN SUPPLEMENT
BLACK CURRANT / BLUEBERRY
5,110 mg FUNCTIONAL INGREDIENTS
88 mg NATURAL CAFFEINE
HEALTH ENERGY

x 3
7.6 fl oz

"This project was a great experience. M13 is a young company full of integrity and a real passion for their product. When a client brings that to the table, the job is 90 percent easier and 100 percent more enjoyable."

—BETTERDAZE PRESS INC.

SUIS SKIN

PROJECT: Suis Skin DESIGN FIRM: BBDK, Inc. CLIENT: Suis Skin
DESIGNER: Duane King ART DIRECTOR: Duane King COPYWRITER:
Duane King FONTS USED: Kursivschrift, Filosofia Italic

"This packaging was developed for an all-natural, organic cosmetics company to embody their simple philosophy of 'loving the skin you're in.' The clean typographic treatment reflects the purity and simplicity of their formulas, while also appealing to consumers who pay careful attention to the ingredients of the products they use."

—BBDK

"Tapio is a premium spirit mixed drink made from all-natural ingredients produced by a young, independent company based in London. Our aim was to reflect their originality in a highly competitive drink market and provide a flexible canvas to build upon as their product range grows. We wanted the design to be playful yet mature and avoid the usual crafty style that natural products often carry. Since it was first launched in 2007, the drink has continued to breed with new flavors and a growing consumer base."

—TRANSFER STUDIO

PROJECT: Tapio DESIGN FIRM: Transfer Studio CLIENT: Tapio Ventures Ltd. DESIGNERS: Falko Grentrup, Valeria Hedman ART DIRECTORS: Falko Grentrup, Valeria Hedman FONTS USED: Amasis, Adabi

TAPIO

BIOGURT

PROJECT: Biogurt **DESIGN FIRM:** Gilberto Sánchez **CLIENT:**
Daniela Campos **DESIGNER:** Gilberto Sánchez **ART DIRECTOR:**
Gilberto Sánchez **COPYWRITER:** Gilberto Sánchez

"The dairy products category has paid particular attention to increasing the interests of consumers into the new 'cosmeto-food' category. A clean, fresh and inviting design with a proper balance between nature and appetite appeal makes the package speak to the feminine market. Using duo-pack's front panel as a billboard, the packaging delivers a great impact to stand out on the shelf."

—GILBERTO SÁNCHEZ

"The goal of this project was to create a high-end men's amenities line. To achieve an upper-scale look for the product, we used modern and clean typography, along with a wood grain label affixed to an aluminum bottle."

—BETH COLLER

PROJECT: Spruce **DESIGNER:** Beth Coller **FONTS USED:** Tall Film (modified slightly), Trade Gothic

SPRUCE

COMME DES GARÇONS EAU DE PARFUM

PROJECT: Comme des Garçons Eau de Parfum DESIGN FIRM: Marc Atlan Design, Inc. CLIENT: Comme des Garçons DESIGNER: Marc Atlan ART DIRECTOR: Marc Atlan PHOTOGRAPHER: Albert Giordan FONT USED: Helvetica

"For Comme des Garçons's first perfume, the packaging had to capture the iconic and pure vision of this distinctive fashion house. The minimalist aesthetic of the package resists convention and specific gender connotation and lends it an almost subversive quality."

—MARC ATLAN DESIGN, INC.

"The design of Odeur 53 is a visual take on an aromatic chemical formula, as if it were concocted in the clinical environment of an experimental lab. Its 53 fragrance components are all cloned odors, and the pack had to reflect this artificial vocabulary, as organized as a periodic table of atomic weights.

The classic vertical volume of the cologne bottle has been knocked onto its side to emphasize the mass and substance of this complex odor."

—MARC ATLAN DESIGN, INC.

ODEUR 53 EAU DE TOILETTE

COMME DES GARÇONS PARFUM S.A. 16 PLACE VENDÔME 75001 PARIS. INGREDIENTS: ALCOHOL DENAT. (65% VOL.), AQUA, PARFUM. CONTENTS: SD ALCOHOL 39-C (65% VOL.), WATER, FRAGRANCE. CET ARTICLE NE PEUT ÊTRE VENDU QUE PAR LES DÉPOSITAIRES AGRÉÉS COMME DES GARÇONS. PRODUCT OF FRANCE.

COMME des GARÇONS

3 488751 405331   e 200 ML. 6.8 FL.OZ.

PROJECT: Comme des Garçons Odeur 53 DESIGN FIRM: Marc Atlan Design, Inc. CLIENT: Comme des Garçons DESIGNER: Marc Atlan ART DIRECTOR: Marc Atlan PHOTOGRAPHER: Albert Giordan FONT USED: Helvetica

COMME DES GARÇONS
ODEUR 53

COMME DES GARÇONS GIFTS AND SAMPLES

PROJECT: Comme des Garçons Gifts & Samples DESIGN FIRM: Marc Atlan Design, Inc. CLIENT: Comme des Garçons Parfums DESIGNER: Marc Atlan
ART DIRECTOR: Marc Atlan PHOTOGRAPHER: Marc Atlan FONT USED: Helvetica

"In these Comme des Garçons special samples sets, oversized plastic wrap incongruously dwarfs the small perfume vials, which are nestled into a copper printed sheet. Metallic colors create a contrast to the functional and technological aspect of these unpretentious arrangements.

The huge fonts printed on the background of the candle and eau de parfum gift pack become distorted and obscured by the encapsulated samples. To underscore the gifts' one-of-a-kind nature, the shrunken plastic crumbles each metallic mini-poster into a unique shape."

—MARC ATLAN DESIGN

METHOD NATURAL MOISTURIZING

PROJECT: Natural Moisturizing Body Care Line **DESIGN FIRM:** Method Products **CLIENT:** Method Products **DESIGNER:** Josh Handy **ART DIRECTOR:** Sally Clarke **PHOTOGRAPHER:** Todd Tankersley **COPYWRITER:** Melissa Sheehan **FONT USED:** Avenir

OLIVE LEAF
NATURAL BODY WASH
SAVON LIQUIDE POUR LE CORPS NATUREL
feuille d'olivier

method 532 mL (18 FL OZ)

"Method's natural moisturizing hand wash, body wash and body bars are made with olive oil and antioxidants like vitamin A and vitamin E to leave your skin so soft that it may just inspire spontaneous nudity. The creamy, soft-touch HDPE and quilted finish of the bottles are intended to reflect this creamy softness and feel at home in your bathroom (or any bathroom, for that matter). The hand wash is labeled with a removable sleeve so it can share in the spontaneous nudity, leaving your bathroom sink looking more like a spa than a supermarket aisle."

—METHOD PRODUCTS

CHAPTER 4
CHARMING

CHARMING: ADORABLE, PLAYFUL, FUN, CUTE, CLEVER, AMUSING, CHEERFUL, PERSONALITY-DRIVEN. THIS SECTION IS ALL ABOUT PACKAGING THAT PUTS A SMILE ON YOUR FACE.

DR STUART'S

PROJECT: Dr Stuart's **DESIGN FIRM:** Pearlfisher **CLIENT:** Only Natural Products Ltd **DESIGNER:** Natalie Chung **COPYWRITER:** Lisa Desforges
FONTS USED: Times, Trade Gothic

"Our redesigned packs focus on the personality of Dr. Stuart, imagining him as an idiosyncratic expert in herbs. This personality is brought to life both visually and verbally, with a surreal illustration for each variant accompanied by a peculiar, but relevant, descriptor. Clean, white space with black typography and a color block bring a fresh modernity to the brand, which has been rebranded under our new Extraordinarily Good Teas strapline. The overall feel redefines Dr Stuart's as a personality-driven brand that successfully combines eccentricity with efficacy."

—PEARLFISHER

"After receiving organic certification, Gulf Pacific Rice needed help bringing a product to the market that had the potential to be more than just another commodity on the shelf. By injecting personality and an aesthetic that resonate with the product and the audience seeking it, Simple Seed became not just food for the table, but food for thought, making the leap from need to want."

—CAPSULE

PROJECT: Simple Seed DESIGN FIRM: Capsule CLIENT: Gulf Pacific Rice DESIGNER: Dan Baggenstoss ART DIRECTOR: Brian Adducci FONTS USED: Clarendon, Consort

SIMPLE SEED

THIS WATER

PROJECT: This Water **DESIGN FIRM:** Pearlfisher **CLIENT:** Innocent Drinks
DESIGNER: Sarah Pidgeon **COPYWRITER:** Lisa Desforges **FONTS USED:**
Helvetica, Futura, Century Gothic

fruit from the trees, **this water**™ from a spring

mango, passion fruit & spring water

this water™ quenches thirsts for a living

blackcurrants & spring water

no treks came from the Alps to bring you **this water**™

lemon, lime & spring water

there are 89 cranberries in every bottle of **this water**™ and 13 raspberries too

cranberries, raspberries & spring water

"The brand was inspired by both the ubiquity and miracle of water. Bright and quirky illustrations combine with hand-scribbled copy to create a bold, fresh, new look. The name was chosen for its versatility and ability to be used as part of personality-driven phrases on- and off-pack. The finished article is a brand that references Innocent, but has the strength and flexibility to succeed as its very own brand."

—PEARLFISHER

OLOVES

PROJECT: Oloves **DESIGN FIRM:** Cowan London **CLIENT:** Brand Stand
Limited **DESIGNER:** Simon Attfield **ART DIRECTOR:** David Pearman
ILLUSTRATORS: Martin Clarke, Stuart Flood **COPYWRITERS:** Simon Attfield,
Gareth Beeson **FONTS USED:** Century Gothic, Helvetica Neue

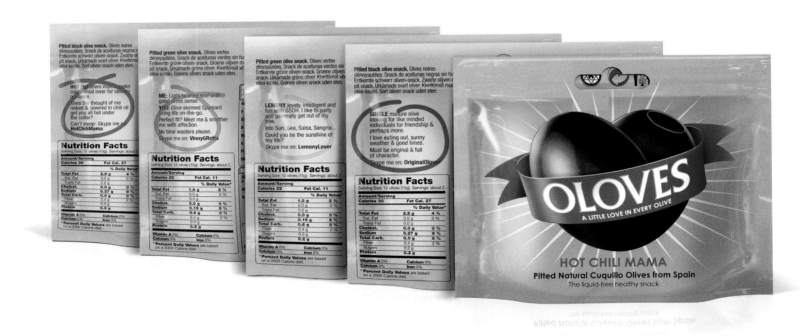

"The redesign focused on giving the brand personality
and making it fun for consumers."

—COWAN LONDON

LIGHT HEARTED VINAIGRETTE
Pitted Green Manzanilla Olives from Spain
The liquid-free healthy snack

HOT CHILI MAMA
Pitted Natural Cuquillo Olives from Spain
The liquid-free healthy snack

LEMONY LOVER
Pitted Green Manzanilla Olives from Spain
The liquid-free healthy snack

THE ORIGINAL
Pitted Natural Cuquillo Olives from Spain
The liquid-free healthy snack

FRUTA DEL DIABLO

PROJECT: Fruta Del Diablo salsa packaging **DESIGN FIRM:** Moxie Sozo
CLIENT: Fruta Del Diablo **DESIGNER:** Nate Dyer **ART DIRECTOR:** Leif Steiner
PHOTOGRAPHER: Laura Kottlowski

"Moxie Sozo wanted to create salsa packaging for Fruta Del Diablo that would distinguish it from everything else on the shelf and establish credibility for an unknown brand. By using hand-drawn illustrations inspired by the woodcuts of Mexican artist José Guadalupe Posada, we were able to lend authenticity to the salsa while reinforcing the product's heritage in traditional Mexican cuisine."

—MOXIE SOZO

HOTDOG

PROJECT: HOTdog **DESIGN FIRM:** Atelier du Presse-Citron **CLIENT:** Fruits & Passion **DESIGNERS:** Suzanne Côté, Jocelyn Laplante **ART DIRECTORS:** Suzanne Côté, Jocelyn Laplante **COLLAGE:** Suzanne Côté, Jocelyn Laplante **PHOTOGRAPHER:** Guy Tessier **ILLUSTRATOR:** Rogé Girard **FONT USED:** Today

"Meet Lulu. She's the star of project 'HOTdog' and the new look for a line of canine-care products developed for Fruits & Passion. We bred our own hound for the concept, using an original illustration by Rogé. Domestico urbanus is a cross between a dachshund and household items—chosen to demonstrate how each product makes dogs more dashing. Bonus: The products' muzzle-shaped bottle caps are made of bouncing rubber for dogs to play with!"

—ATELIER DU PRESSE-CITRON

EMILY'S CHOCOLATES

PROJECT: Emily's Chocolates packaging **DESIGN FIRM:** Hornall Anderson
CLIENT: AMES International Inc. **DESIGNERS:** Kathy Saito, Sonja Max, Henry
Yiu, Yuri Shvets **ART DIRECTORS:** Jack Anderson, Kathy Saito **COPYWRITER:**
Pamela Mason Davey

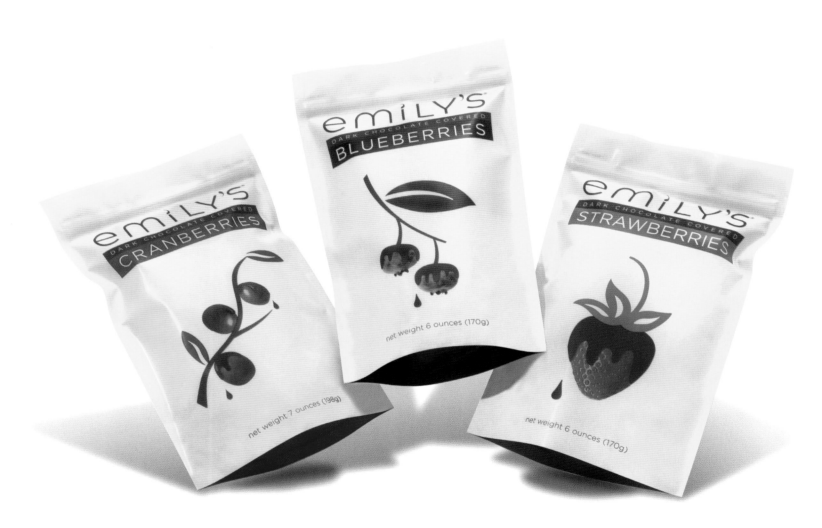

"AMES International Inc. approached us with the need to address their flagship line of Emily's chocolate-covered fruit and nut products. Their goal was to build a strong national brand around Emily's, strengthen existing retail relationships and expand their distribution into specialty retail and discount stores. We began with identifying a color palette that was unique in the space and paired it with a distinctive and playful illustration style. The new packaging contributed to a dramatic uptick in sales and is directly attributed to entry into Walmart, Target, Costco and numerous specialty food retailers."

—HORNALL ANDERSON

RINGNES SOMMERØL

PROJECT: Ringnes Sommerøl "Summer Beer" **DESIGN FIRM**: Scandinavian
Design Group **CLIENT**: Ringnes Brewery **DESIGNER**: Eirik Seu Stokkmo
ART DIRECTOR: Eirik Seu Stokkmo **COPYWRITER**: Eirik Seu Stokkmo
FONT USED: Georgia

"Ringnes Sommerøl (Summer Beer) is a limited seasonal product from one of the main beer producers in Norway. The limited life of the product and the young target allow the design to be more fun and less durable, focusing on being different and fresh. The abstract shapes making up the word 'Sommerøl' wrap around the can, giving a sense of lightness that suits the summer vibe. The golden colors ensure that the design stays closer to the world of beer, and the light gold gives the beer a sense of coldness needed on a warm summer day."

—SCANDINAVIAN DESIGN GROUP

METHOD BABY LINE

PROJECT: Method baby line **DESIGN FIRM:** Method Products **CLIENT:** Method Products **DESIGNER:** Josh Handy **ART DIRECTOR:** Sally Clarke **PHOTOGRAPHER:** Todd Tankersley **COPYWRITER:** Melissa Sheehan **FONT USED:** Avenir

"The hair and body wash has a cap that doubles as a handy rinsing cup, helping you gently cleanse delicate skin without making a mess. The body lotion is easy to pump (even with one hand—we know how it is), so your lil' one will stay baby soft all day. Rounding out the mix, the bubbly bath is an easy-to-use, bottom-dispensing bottle (yes, one-hand use again—seriously, we know how it is), cleverly disguised as a little creature. Your little creature will love it so much you probably won't even want to recycle it, even though they're all recyclable."

—METHOD

TESCO SMOOTHIES

PROJECT: Tesco Smoothies **DESIGN FIRM:** Pemberton & Whitefoord **CLIENT:** Tesco **DESIGNER:** Liway Skelding-Jones **ART DIRECTOR:** Simon Pemberton **ILLUSTRATOR:** Gilly Lovegrove **FONTS USED:** Helvetica Neue, FG Tor

TESCO
RASPBERRY & BLUEBERRY
SMOOTHIE

TESCO
ORANGE, MANGO
& PINEAPPLE SMOOTHIE

TESCO
APPLE & BLACKCURRANT
SMOOTHIE

THIS IS HOW OUR LOVELY SMOOTHIES ARE MADE...

EACH 250ML CONTAINS AT LEAST 2 PORTIONS OF FRUIT.

"The objective was to create a strong point of difference in the chiller cabinet by using iconic, simple graphics in a normally photographic-dominated area, and by creating naive illustrations to communicate the goodness of the product."

—PEMBERTON & WHITEFOORD

AROMATHERAPY INTERVENTIONS

PROJECT: Aromatherapy Interventions **DESIGN FIRM:** JR McKee Communications Group **CLIENT:** JR McKee Communications Group **DESIGNERS:** Don Stephenson, Dustin Van Wechel **ART DIRECTORS:** John McKee, Dustin Van Wechel **COPYWRITERS:** John McKee, Ross McKee **FONTS USED:** Clarendon, Helvetica Neue Light Extended

"The key design problem was attempting to balance the need for a cohesive brand image while expressing—at a glance—the individuality of each of the 25 candle concepts in the line."

—JR MCKEE COMMUNICATIONS GROUP

panic attack™*

Aromatherapy indicated for general fears of job loss, blind dates, computer viruses and STDs.

Aromatherapy
INTERVENTIONS™

ESSENCE OF FRANKINCENSE HELPS COUNTER PANIC, TRAUMA AND DRAMA.

Pure Burn Soy Wax Candle

panic attack™*

Aromatherapy for general fears of job loss, computer viruses, blind dates, and WMDs.

therapists choice™*

If your moods change faster than you can light a match, this self-diagnosing layered candle will help keep you on track

Aromatherapy

birthday panic™*

You have yet to save the planet, surf an endless Summer or party like a rock star.

Aromatherapy
INTERVENTIONS™

ESSENCE OF FRANKINCENSE LESSENS RESTLESS ANXIETY.

Pure Burn Soy Wax Candle

birthday panic™*

You have yet to save the planet, surf an endless Summer or party like a rock star.

JONATHAN CRISP

PROJECT: Jonathan Crisp **DESIGN FIRM:** Ziggurat Brands **CLIENT:** Natural Crisps Ltd. **ART DIRECTOR:** Allison Miguel **FONTS USED:** Bespoke, Franklin Gothic Condensed, ITC Stone Serif Medium

"Our challenge was to redesign the Jonathan Crisp brand, clearly positioning it as a premium brand of crisps. The packs were only sold in niche markets, so developing a brand that could grow through distribution and also make an impact in an extremely competitive market was key. Not wanting to mimic premium brands, such as Kettle or Tyrells, the solution had to be original and engaging. The idea was to exaggerate the idea of premium by positioning the brand as 'Crisps for Snobs.' Borrowing from the great British satirical tradition, we created a set of upper-class caricatures to depict each flavor, and the copy on the back of each pack is scripted to read like a page out of *Who's Who*."

—ZIGGURAT BRANDS

COCA-COLA LIGHT PLUS

PROJECT: Coca-Cola Light Plus visual identity system and packaging **DESIGN FIRM:** Office: Jason Schulte Design, Inc. **CLIENT:** The Coca-Cola Company **DESIGNERS:** Jason Schulte, Nicole Flores **CREATIVE DIRECTOR:** Jason Schulte **FONTS USED:** Twentieth Century, custom

"For Coca-Cola Light Plus, a soft drink fortified with vitamins and minerals, we established the visual language, packaging and guidelines to help the global Coke team manage the brand's launch in each local market. Plus is about doing what's good for you and indulging in what you love, so we worked to communicate that balance."

—OFFICE

EARBUDEEZ

PROJECT: earBudeez **DESIGN FIRM:** JDA, Inc. **CLIENT:** Audiovox Corporation
DESIGNERS: Dean Kojima, Jerome Calleja **ART DIRECTORS:** David Jensen,
Jerome Calleja **CREATIVE DIRECTOR:** Dave Jensen **ILLUSTRATORS:** Dean Kojima,
Jerome Calleja **COPYWRITER:** Carter Crimm **FONT USED:** Helvetica Neue

"The goal of this project was to make the Mobility Expanded brand stand out on the shelf by giving the packaging visual impact. Since there aren't many differences between the brands, we came up with the concept to create characters for each ear-bud color. We used the earbuds as the eyes and placed them in different positions to give each character a different personality."

—JDA, INC.

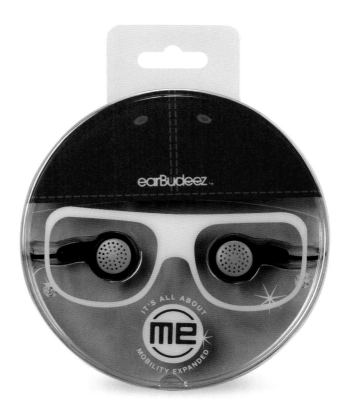

LITTLE ME ORGANICS

PROJECT: Little Me Organics **DESIGN FIRM:** R Design **CLIENT:**
Floraroma Ltd. **DESIGNER:** Charlotte Hayes **ART DIRECTOR:** Dave Richmond
FONTS USED: Baskerville, Gill Sans

"The brief was to redesign the packs to be aesthetically pleasing to mothers and to
stand out in an extremely competitive market, while communicating the organic
benefits and origins of the product. We achieved this by using a largely decorative
floral illustration incorporating the brand identity with the use of bold, bright colors, which emulate children's book illustrations."

—R DESIGN

"We created a branding system that communicates the emotions associated with enjoying dessert. The name and identity are sophisticated yet playful, like the client's delicious products. Cakes, cookies, truffles and desserts will sell themselves a lot of times. HK simply put the icing on the cake."

—HARTUNGKEMP

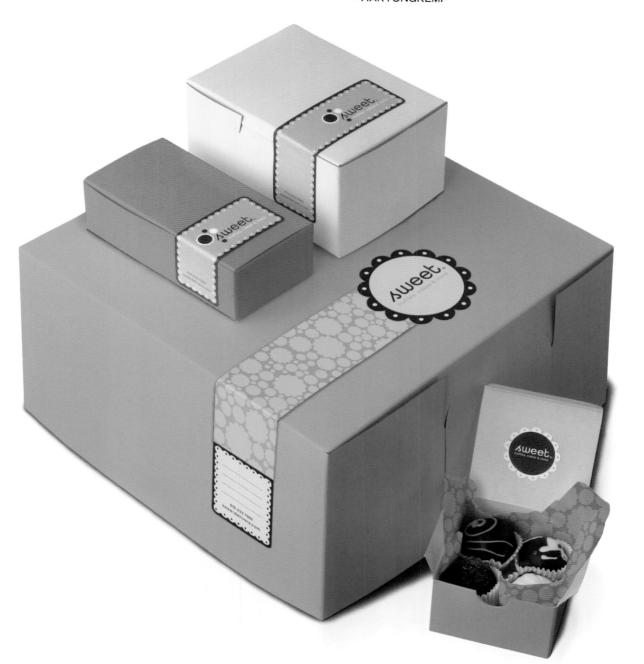

PROJECT: Sweet DESIGN FIRM: HartungKemp CLIENT: Route 29 DESIGNER: Devon Adrian ART DIRECTOR: Stefan Hartung PHOTOGRAPHER: HartungKemp FONTS USED: Customized Chalet, Suburban

SWEET

LET_IT_GROW

PROJECT: Let_it_grow bottles DESIGN FIRM: Let_it_grow CLIENT:
Let_it_grow DESIGNER: Danilo Tranquilli ART DIRECTOR: Danilo Tranquilli
PHOTOGRAPHER: Manoel Marques COPYWRITER: Juliana Seabra
FONT USED: Baskerville

"We wanted to create a gift for clients, partners and friends that could say more about us and our ideas—something remarkable and different from the usual calendars and posters.

We took 100 bottles of wine that could go to the garbage, and painted all of them in a white color. After this first step, we decide to create 100 drawings, exclusive and unique for each one.

To keep the surprise, we decided to cover it with a black plastic (those used to sell grains of coffee) in a vacuum process. Inside the packaging, there is a little tag explaining the project.

We decided to use wine bottles because they're an icon of celebration and friendship for us. The concept of the vacuum plastic bag is, 'Don't suffocate creativity, just let it free.'"

—LET_IT_GROW

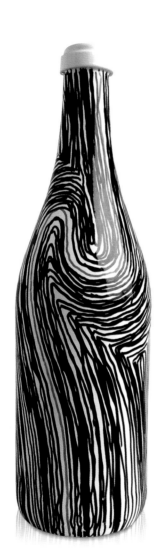

PETITE FRANCE

PROJECT: Petite France identity and package design **DESIGN FIRM:** Beckmans College of Design (Stockholm) **CLIENT:** Petite France **DESIGNERS:** Zorica Radovic, Petter Hanberger **ART DIRECTORS:** Zorica Radovic, Petter Hanberger **PHOTOGRAPHERS:** Zorica Radovic, Petter Hanberger **COPYWRITERS:** Zorica Radovic, Petter Hanberger **FONT USED:** Gill Sans

"Petite France is a bakery in Stockholm. They are well known in the neighborhood for their high quality and genuine passion for pastries. We found the word 'meet' relevant to represent Petite France—the dough meets the baker, the customer meets the café, the bread meets the customer, France meets Sweden, etc. The result was a number of patterns meeting in a Petite France patchwork."

—ZORICA RADOVIC, PETTER HANBERGER

ROUTE 29 EASTER LINE

PROJECT: Route 29 Easter Line **DESIGN FIRM:** HartungKemp **CLIENT:** Route 29
DESIGNER: Devon Adrian **ART DIRECTOR:** Stefan Hartung **PHOTOGRAPHER:**
HartungKemp **FONTS USED:** DIN, Wendy

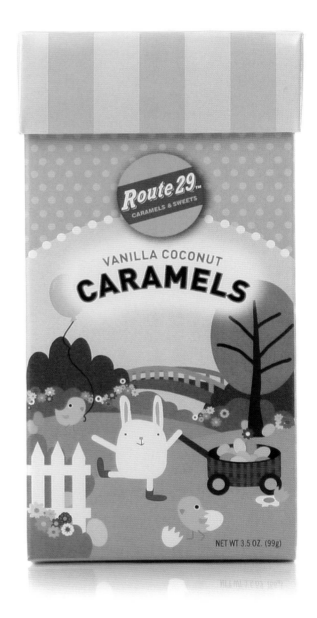

"Each keepsake package features bunnies and chicks frolicking through a scene sure to be a welcome addition to any Easter basket. Those little illustrations have made it fun to evolve the Route 29 brand with each new holiday season."

—HARTUNGKEMP

"Taste these hot-'n'-bothered, gooey-gourmet, let-the-chips-fall-where-they-may, delivered-to-your-door cookies and mere flowers will wilt in comparison. Spunk mixed up the logo, package, website, stationery, T-shirts, promotional video and cookie car design, baking a brand that appeals to an audience hungry for sophisticated quality. Tank Goodness is served up as a gift, a reward, an escape and an indulgence. A true mom-pop-'n'-sons cottage industry, Tank Goodness has become so successful, they're currently pursuing partnership and franchise opportunities."

—SPUNK DESIGN MACHINE

TANK GOODNESS COOKIES

PROJECT: Tank Goodness Cookies **DESIGN FIRM:** Spunk Design Machine
CLIENT: Tank Goodness Cookies **DESIGNERS:** Steve Jockisch, Jason Walzer
ART DIRECTOR: Jeff Johnson **PHOTOGRAPHER:** Mickey Smith **COPYWRITER:**
Phil Calvit **FONTS USED:** Bryant, custom

"Today, it is increasingly acceptable for women to be having casual sex. However, many women do not carry protection. Durex Fantasy is a range of condoms intended to encourage women to buy and carry a condom—'because you never know.' The greatest challenge in the design process was creating something that women could buy and carry without fear of being judged. However, the packaging shouldn't disguise the fact that it is a condom, as this merely conforms to the notion that women should feel embarrassed about carrying condoms.

The outcome was successful because it acknowledges the fact that women are just as sexually aware as men. While suggestive, the packaging is neither brash nor vulgar."

—PHILIP SKINNER

DUREX FANTASY

PROJECT: Durex Fantasy **DESIGNER:** Philip Skinner
CLIENT: Durex

DANU HAIR CARE

PROJECT: DANU hair care **DESIGN FIRM:** Vigor **CLIENT:** 5th Avenue Salon
DESIGNER: Joseph Szala **ART DIRECTOR:** Joseph Szala **COPYWRITERS:**
Joseph Szala, Jason Bowser **FONT USED:** Archer

"Crafting a brand that would speak to new mothers was a challenge I welcomed
with open arms. Learning about the emotional and mental changes a woman faces
upon pregnancy and birth was integral in designing a product that hit the mark."

—VIGOR

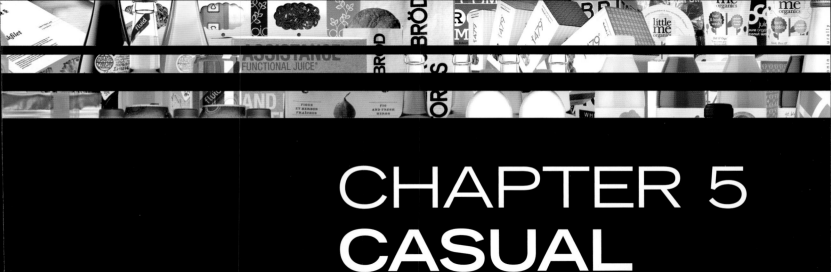

CHAPTER 5
CASUAL

SILVER JOE'S

PROJECT: Silver Joe's coffee tin **DESIGN FIRM:** C3 Brandworks, Inc. **CLIENT:** Silver Joe's Coffee Company **DESIGNER:** Cameron Clement **ART DIRECTOR:** Cameron Clement **PHOTOGRAPHER:** Steve Jones **COPYWRITER:** Cameron Clement **FONTS USED:** Univers, Trade Gothic, PT Script Zephyr

"A challenge in the Silver Joe's project was to create a container unlike any other for coffee—something stackable, reversible and versatile. The package communicates with the shopper from three sides, and it allows high pack out efficiencies with a butterfly arrangement. This also allows for many expressions on the shelf."

—C3 BRANDWORKS, INC.

FRESCA

PROJECT: Fresca DESIGN FIRM: Duffy & Partners CLIENT: The Coca-Cola Company DESIGNERS: Ken Sakurai, George Katz ART DIRECTOR: Dan Olson PHOTOGRAPHER: Martin Wonacott FONTS USED: Stratum 1 Regular, Stratum 1 Bold, Myriad Regular

"The revitalization of the Fresca brand was about changing a 'child of the 1960s' into a sophisticated adult soft drink for today. The crisp, citrus taste profile with no calories added up to the perfect drink for an active adult audience. Our brief was to create a brand language that would reflect the unique taste and appeal to this audience."

—DUFFY & PARTNERS

HINT

PROJECT: Hint DESIGN FIRM: Bluelounge Design DESIGNERS: Doris Kao, Diana Sopha ART DIRECTOR: Melissa Sunjaya PHOTOGRAPHERS: Jason Ware, Dominic Symons COPYWRITER: Stuart Frolic FONTS USED: Neutraface, DIN

"This was a complete branding design project, from the creation of the Hint name to the concept of 'a hint of flavor,' using floating fruit on transparent labels with witty copy."

—BLUELOUNGE DESIGN

WAITROSE PICKLES

PROJECT: Waitrose Pickles **DESIGN FIRM:** Pearlfisher **CLIENT:** Waitrose Ltd.
DESIGNER: Mark Christou **FONTS USED:** custom

"The best ideas are always the simplest, and the hard work is in making it look effortless. In this case, the product sold itself and didn't need beautifying via the conventions of false food photography. Instead, we revealed the pickles in their gloriously natural state through the glass jar and used bold, colorful typography artfully squished together to reflect the abundant and flavorsome products inside the jars to create individual desire and a stunning range on the shelf."

—PEARLFISHER

"Our challenge was to create a new distinctive brand image for Bürgen, while communicating its new positioning: 'harnessing the power of nature.' The new design shifted consumer perception of the brand, and Bürgen is now leading within the positive health bread category. The design has fundamentally improved shelf impact and clearly communicates the brand's positive health message."

—ZIGGURAT BRANDS

BÜRGEN

PROJECT: Bürgen **DESIGN FIRM:** Ziggurat Brands **CLIENT:** Allied Bakeries
DESIGNER: Andy Audsley **ART DIRECTOR:** Allison Miguel **FONTS USED:**
Frutiger, custom

"The challenge for the graphic design was to translate the freshness of the Jamba Juice in-store experience to a shelf-stable package sold from a retail grocery store. Additionally, we wanted to create a graphic design approach that worked synergistically with the unique bottle structure."

—DEUTSCH DESIGN WORKS, INC.

JAMBA JUICE

PROJECT: Jamba Juice line **DESIGN FIRMS:** Deutsch Design Works, Inc. (graphics), Product Ventures Ltd. (structure) **CLIENT:** Nestlé Beverage Company **DESIGN DIRECTOR:** Erika Krieger **CREATIVE DIRECTOR:** Jason Abreu **STRUCTURAL DESIGNERS:** Jon Lee, Peter Clarke **COPYWRITER:** Sue Greenberg **FONTS USED:** Chevin, Blockhead, Handy Sans

FANTA

PROJECT: Fanta visual identity system, identity and packaging DESIGN FIRM: Office: Jason Schulte Design, Inc. CLIENT: The Coca-Cola Company DESIGNERS: Jason Schulte, Rob Alexander, Gaelyn Mangrum, Nicole Flores, Jeff Bucholtz CREATIVE DIRECTOR: Jason Schulte PHOTOGRAPHER: Pat Boemer FONT USED: Frankfurter

"We created a new visual identity for Fanta, including a global design strategy, logo, packaging system and point of sale marketing. The visual vocabulary is rooted in Fanta's orange heritage and embodies the brand's imaginative, exuberant spirit. A range of branding elements allow the Fanta team to emphasize different messages, resulting in a system that is flexible enough to work in more than 180 countries around the world."

—OFFICE

IZZE

PROJECT: IZZE soda packaging **DESIGN FIRM:** TDA Advertising & Design **CLIENT:** IZZE **DESIGNERS:** Teresa Forrester, Rich Rodgers **ART DIRECTOR:** Thomas Dooley **FONT USED:** Trade Gothic

"IZZE was one of the first packaging designs we created entirely from scratch. It was the direct result of our unhappiness with cluttered packaging design and packaging designed to look natural that only tended to blend in with all other natural packaging. IZZE looked fresh and natural without having to say it. It also allowed a whole new audience—who could care less about natural—to enjoy it."

—TDA ADVERTISING & DESIGN

WAITROSE CAT LITTER

DESIGN FIRM: Turner Duckworth CLIENT: Waitrose Ltd. CREATIVE
DIRECTORS: David Turner, Bruce Duckworth DESIGNER: Jamie McCathie
PHOTOGRAPHER: Phil Cook ILLUSTRATORS: John Geary, Peter Ruane
RETOUCHING: Peter Ruane FONT USED: Bliss

"While cleaning out the litter box is an everyday chore for feline-owning consumers, the design solution for the range found its inspiration in the way most cat lovers treat their pets—not as an 'animal,' but as one of the family. The front of the pack became a door with a customized plaque with the cat drawn in the style of the man and woman symbols seen on toilet doors in public places. Only the best is good enough for Tiddles."

—TURNER DUCKWORTH

STARBUCKS DOUBLESHOT

PROJECT: Doubleshot **DESIGN FIRM:** Duffy & Partners **CLIENT:** Starbucks
DESIGNERS: David Mashburn, Jeff Hale **ART DIRECTOR:** Dan Olson

"What was exciting about this challenge was creating a
bold, artist-driven design for Starbucks Doubleshot that
would transcend cultural barriers."

—DUFFY & PARTNERS

18 RABBITS

PROJECT: 18 Rabbits Granola **DESIGN FIRM:** STROHL **CLIENT:** Alison Bailey Vercruysse **DESIGNERS:** Eric Strohl, Christine Strohl **FONTS USED:** custom drawn and modified faces

"When Divinely D'lish, a beloved San Francisco granola brand, decided to expand their demographic, we started at square one, devising a more authentic brand story, crafting a unique company name, as well as creating a new brand aesthetic across all products.

Based on the founder's own experiences as a child raising eighteen pet rabbits, the goal was to make the visual identity more distinct and easily recognizable, as well as fun. The bright color palette works as a labeling system, allowing the customers to easily identify their favorite flavor on the cluttered supermarket shelves."

—STROHL

U HYDRATION

PROJECT: U Hydration **DESIGN FIRM:** Moxie Sozo **CLIENT:** Nuun & Company
DESIGNERS: Stephanie Shank, Charles Bloom **ART DIRECTOR:** Leif Steiner
PHOTOGRAPHER: Laura Kottlowski **FONTS USED:** Chalet, DIN, Century Gothic

"Nuun wanted to expand their product line to offer a healthy hydration alternative for everyday life."

—MOXIE SOZO

"[Nuun] developed U, a low-sugar, low-calorie option for hydration. Their primary target included women between the ages of 25 and 40 who shop at Whole Foods, practice yoga and are environmentally conscientious. Their packaging needed to stand out on the shelves without being overt, suggest an active lifestyle without alienating casual consumers, and justify U's higher price point. Moxie Sozo created packaging with a feminine feel, imagery with a subtle reference to yoga and dance, and a layered design to give it a quiet elegance."

—MOXIE SOZO

HONEYDROP

PROJECT: Honeydrop **DESIGN FIRM:** Pearlfisher **CLIENT:** Honeydrop **DESIGNER:** Mark Christou **CREATIVE DIRECTOR:** Lisa Simpson **COPYWRITER:** Arnava Asen

"The Bee is the heart of the brand and the first thing the consumer is drawn to on the pack. It sets a friendly and approachable tone by working in conjunction with each product benefit: Bee Good, Bee Alive, Bee Calm, Bee Strong. This makes up a distinct language for the brand that translates beyond packaging across the Deluxe Honeydrop brand. The friendly tone continues on the side-of-pack story, which further emphasizes Honeydrop's sweet personality. The website brings to life the Bee, and the brand, by using the icon to tie the pages and brand information together, still retaining the simplicity from the pack design."

—PEARLFISHER

"Our challenge was to design a natural line of products that would resonate with everyday guys who have specific grooming needs and concerns. Our design also needed to convey the environmental benefits of using Aveda, as well as the global environmental commitments of Aveda as a company."

—DUFFY & PARTNERS

PROJECT: Aveda Men Pure-Formance DESIGN FIRM: Duffy & Partners CLIENT: Aveda DESIGNERS: Sam Sherman, Joseph Duffy IV ART DIRECTOR: Dan Olson COPYWRITER: Russ Stark FONTS USED: DIN Neuzeit Grotesk LT, FF DIN Medium

AVEDA MEN PURE-FORMANCE

ENVIGA

PROJECT: Enviga identity and packaging **DESIGN FIRM:** Office: Jason Schulte Design, Inc. **CLIENT:** Beverage Partners Worldwide **DESIGNER:** Jason Schulte **CREATIVE DIRECTOR:** Jason Schulte **FONTS USED:** Futura, Trade Gothic

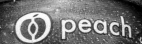

FASTACHI

PROJECT: Fastachi brand facelift **DESIGN FIRM:** OVO **CLIENT:** Souren
Etyemezian **DESIGNER:** Toni Oberholzer **ART DIRECTOR:** Toni Oberholzer
PHOTOGRAPHER: Tanya Rosen Jones **COPYWRITER:** Toni Lansbury
FONT USED: Nuri

"Beauty and freshness were the prerequisites when rebranding the preeminent nut purveyor Fastachi. Handcrafted quality and distinction move consumers to sample and repurchase premium food products. Special consideration was given to creating packages worthy of gift giving."

—OVO

DRENCH

PROJECT: Drench **DESIGN FIRM:** Jones Knowles Ritchie **CLIENT:** Britvic Soft Drinks **DESIGNER:** Robert Brooks **ART DIRECTOR:** Glenn Kiernan

FONT USED: Clarendon

100% clear, crisp spring water

drenc

helps you stay mentally and physically hydrated
stay hydrated, stay drenched!

"We wanted to offer a conventional product with a progressive tone of voice. We aimed to break with category conventions (images of mountains, etc., to suggest the waters' provenance) choosing instead to present a simpler design built around the brand's striking name. The word mark is oversized, and this bold abstraction has given the pack great standout on the shelf among an often visually busy competitive set. The design's simplicity and abstraction also play well with the brand's proposition: 'Brains that are well hydrated work better.'"

—JONES KNOWLES RITCHIE

"When asked to consider how to present our client's honey in an attractive way, we decided to go beyond mere packaging label design and produce something unique and wholly 'on brand.' We thought it would be a nice idea if the whole process of buying honey was more cyclical. You buy the honey, eat the honey, knock a hole in the specially designed bottom of the pot and grow new flowers for the bees to visit, who then go make honey, you buy the honey, you eat the honey … you get the idea.

The clay pot held a true pound of honey and was also great in the hand in terms of weight and texture. The cork lid was designed with a recess in the lid to aid with stacking, but also to place your pot on to avoid water marks if it later lived on the windowsill growing new flowers."

—THE PARTNERS

STANLEY HONEY

PROJECT: Stanley Honey Pots **DESIGN FIRM:** The Partners (Design Consultants) Ltd. **CLIENT:** Stanley Honey **DESIGNER:** Dana Robertson
PHOTOGRAPHER: The Partners (Design Consultants) Ltd.

FRESH'N FRUITY

PROJECT: Fresh'n Fruity Yogurt **DESIGN FIRM:** Dow Design Ltd. **CLIENT:** Fonterra Brands NZ, Ltd. **DESIGNER:** Andrew Sparrow **ART DIRECTOR:** Donna McCourt **ILLUSTRATORS:** Grant Reed, Leonie Whyte **INKS:** CMYK and two special mix inks **PRINTING:** Gravure **FONTS:** Vintage, Subway Black, handcrafted logo

"The brief required Fresh'n Fruity to affirm its leadership position in the category. The trademarked imagery will keep Fresh'n Fruity ahead of the pack, while making it easy for yogurt lovers to find their favorite flavor in the supermarket."

—DOW DESIGN LTD.

CHAPTER 5

UGLY PIZZA

PROJECT: UGLY Pizza **DESIGN FIRM:** Vibrandt **CLIENT:** The Schwan
Food Company **DESIGNER:** Karen Cole **ART DIRECTOR:** Carrie Cummins
PHOTOGRAPHER: Alan Newnham **COPYWRITER:** Chris Reay **FONT
USED:** Amasis MT Std

"Launching initially in pizzas, UGLY—developed by Windsor-based brand design
agency Vibrandt—embraces the rising trend for natural, honest food and the notion
that genuinely good food is all about taste and quality, not just the way it looks."

—VIBRANDT

SOPOCANI 100% JUICE

PROJECT: Sopocani 100% Juice DESIGN FIRM: Peter Gregson Studio

CLIENT: Monastery Sopocani Serbia DESIGNERS: Jovan Trkulja, Marijana Zaric

ART DIRECTOR: Jovan Trkulja PHOTOGRAPHER: Igor Ilic

"We designed a new brandmark and packaging: bottles for juices and jars for Serbian delectable products. All the products are organic and natural, and made in a monastery in Sopocani. The label is handwritten, exemplifying the spirit of the product."

—PETER GREGSON STUDIO

COCO JUICE

PROJECT: CoCo Juice **DESIGN FIRM**: Blue Marlin Brand Design Ltd **CLIENT**: Dr. Antonio Martin **DESIGNER**: David Jenkins **ART DIRECTOR**: Martin Grimer **PHOTOGRAPHER**: Andy Seymour **COPYWRITER**: Ed Woodcock

"Dr. Martin's problem was this: He had a groundbreaking range of products that retailers struggled to understand. Our response? A new brand identity that communicated his expertise in coconut biology, a new brand architecture, and a packaging design that lent coherence to a range of products with hugely varying characteristics and benefits. After the redesign, stockers went nuts. Retailers who had previously turned him down fought for the privilege of launching the new range."

—BLUE MARLIN BRAND DESIGN LTD

CHAPTER 6
NOSTALGIC

NOSTALGIC: VINTAGE, CLASSIC, RETRO, ANTIQUE, OLD-FASHIONED, REMINISCENT. THIS SECTION IS ALL ABOUT PACKAGING THAT REMINDS YOU OF ANOTHER TIME.

SULTRY SALLY

PROJECT: Sultry Sally Potato Chips **DESIGN FIRM:** The Creative Method **CLIENT:** Potato Magic Australia Pty Ltd. **DESIGNER:** Tony Ibbotson **ART DIRECTOR:** Tony Ibbotson **ILLUSTRATOR:** Mark Sofilas **COPYWRITERS:** Martin Pick, Julian Canny **FONTS USED:** Script Bold MT, Helvetica Neue, Freehand 521

"Sultry Sally is a new range of low-fat, high-flavor potato chips. Varga Girl-style illustrations from the 1940s were created as the focus and core idea for the packs as they gave Sally immediate personality and attitude and stand out from existing products on the market. The product price point was at a premium, so the quality, attention to detail and classic style were required to reflect that. Sally is illustrated interacting with each flavor in a different way; this gives good flavor differentiation, while Sally herself is a great link between all the packs in the range."

—THE CREATIVE METHOD

"Ten years ago, Williams-Sonoma introduced its own line of peppermint bark, a holiday tradition for many of their loyal shoppers. In the past ten years, dozens of retailers have attempted to duplicate this holiday favorite. To celebrate the 10th anniversary of the original peppermint bark, Williams-Sonoma wanted to create a commemorative keepsake tin that communicates the premium quality and nostalgia of this seasonal favorite."

—PHILIPPEBECKER

WILLIAMS-SONOMA PEPPERMINT BARK

PROJECT: Williams-Sonoma 10th Anniversary Peppermint Bark **DESIGN FIRM:** PhilippeBecker **CLIENT:** Williams-Sonoma, Inc. **DESIGNERS:** Nikki Allen, Miriko Muto **ART DIRECTOR:** Andrew Otto **ILLUSTRATOR:** Steve Noble **FONTS USED:** Copperplate Gothic, Script MT Bold, Serifa Bold Condensed BT

ART HOME

PROJECT: Art Home DESIGN FIRM: orangetango CLIENT: Fruits & Passion FONTS USED: Helvetica Neue, Clarendon

"This range of environmentally friendly cleaning products takes a vintage spin—a return to more sustainable, authentic packaging. We used a raw finish, in contrast with more subtle scents. The purity of the design and transparency of the package parallel the purpose—keeping things clean! This line replaces pine and lemon with more particular scents. We crafted a brand name that conveys all of these ideas."

—ORANGETANGO

McCRAW'S CONFECTIONS

PROJECT: McCraw's Confections DESIGN FIRM: Tractorbeam CLIENT: McCraw's Confections DESIGNER: Craig Skinner ART DIRECTOR: Craig Skinner CREATIVE DIRECTOR: Jeff Barfoot ILLUSTRATORS: Craig Skinner, Jeff Barfoot COPYWRITER: Craig Skinner FONTS USED: Collier Heading, Knockout, Clarendon

"This rebrand project was so successful the owner embezzled millions of dollars and fled the country. No joke. Unfortunately, the owner really did run off with the profits and bankrupt the company, leaving everyone unpaid and market agreements unfulfilled."

—TRACTORBEAM

WAITROSE BREADSTICKS

PROJECT: Breadsticks **DESIGN FIRM:** Turner Duckworth **CLIENT:** Waitrose Ltd.
DESIGNER: Mark Waters **PHOTOGRAPHER:** Andy Grimshaw **RETOUCHER:**
Peter Ruane **ARTWORKER:** Reuben James **FONTS USED:** Futura, Script MT Bold

"Waitrose briefed us to create a new identity for their range of breadsticks. The line
had been underperforming, due to lack of visibility within the store.

Our solution was to focus on the Italian heritage of the breadsticks and educate
consumers about the difference between grissini (everyday and kids love them)
and Torinesi (pre-dinner party nibble plus additional ingredients). This was achieved
by the use of actual-size photography of the product against a distinctly rustic
graphic background, and telling consumers what the product is in large type."

—TURNER DUCKWORTH

"The idea was to create a brand of wine that shared that same boldness and spirit of a Hatch Show Print poster."

—THREE THIEVES

PROJECT: The Show wine labels DESIGN FIRM: Hatch Show Print

CLIENT: Three Thieves DESIGNER: Brad Vetter ART DIRECTOR: John Benson

FONTS USED: Hatch wood block letters, Aachen Bold, Rosewood

THE SHOW

LOVEJOY VODKA

PROJECT: Lovejoy Vodka **DESIGN FIRM:** ID Branding **CLIENT:** Integrity Spirits **DESIGNER:** Jared Milam **ART DIRECTOR:** Jared Milam **COPYWRITER:** Charla Adams **CREATIVE DIRECTOR:** Doug Lowell **FONTS USED:** custom

"Integrity Spirits came to us with the desire to make a small-batch, handcrafted vodka in Portland, Oregon. We worked with them to create a name that embodied the spirit of both Portland and of vodka in general. (Lovejoy was a pioneer settler of Portland, and there is a street and park named after him there. And love and joy seem integral to the vodka experience.) We chose the bottle shape and designed a series of four labels to be released at the same time for the regular vodka, and a fifth label for the Hazelnut Vodka, allowing customers to choose the design that best fit their mood or the occasion."

—ID BRANDING

YOU SMELL

PROJECT: You Smell **DESIGN FIRM:** Megan Cummins **CLIENT:** None (student project) **DESIGNER:** Megan Cummins **ART DIRECTOR:** Megan Cummins **PHOTOGRAPHER:** Megan Cummins **COPYWRITER:** Megan Cummins **FONTS USED:** Hand-drawn text, Big Caslon, Bickham Script Pro, Eccentric Std, Ecuyer DAX

"Packaging should be experimental, taking into account every detail, from where your thumb goes to open it, to the timing between viewing sides. There's a rhythm to package design; we just have to find the visuals that go along with it."

—MEGAN CUMMINS

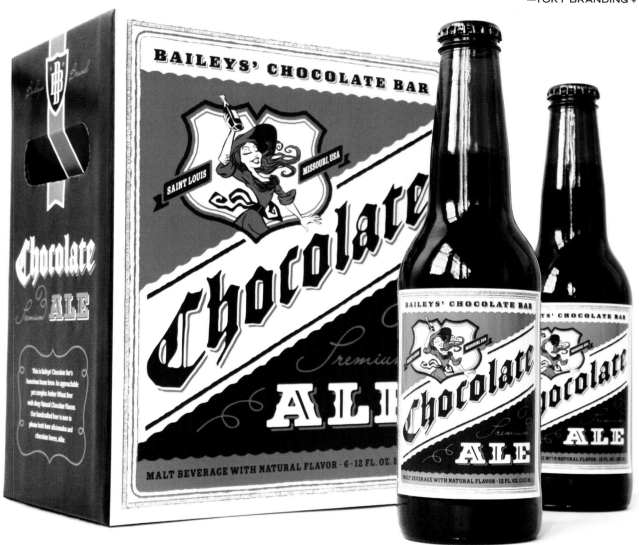

"Baileys' Chocolate Bar is a high-end eating and drinking establishment that serves amazing desserts and cheeses. This is Baileys' Chocolate Bar's luxurious house brew, a handcrafted amber wheat ale with deep, natural, chocolate flavors."

—TOKY BRANDING + DESIGN

BAILEYS' CHOCOLATE ALE

PROJECT: Baileys' Chocolate Ale **DESIGN FIRM:** TOKY Branding + Design
CLIENT: Baileys' Chocolate Bar **DESIGNER:** Travis Brown **CREATIVE DIRECTOR:**
Eric Thoelke **COPYWRITER:** Geoff Story **FONTS USED:** Ironmonger Black,
Lainie Day, Zebrawood, PL Davison Americana, custom blackletter typeface

WILLIAMS-SONOMA QUICK BREAD MIXES

PROJECT: Williams-Sonoma quick bread mixes DESIGN FIRM: PhilippeBecker CLIENT: Williams-Sonoma, Inc. DESIGNERS: Coco Qiu, Barkha Wadia ART DIRECTOR: Philippe Becker FONTS USED: Goudy, Garamond, Trade Gothic, custom

"The goal was to create a visually consistent product line while creating unique personalities for each variety of these super premium bread mixes. We were going for a more traditional, handcrafted look to capture the nostalgia of a time when baking from scratch was a part of our everyday lives."

—PHILIPPEBECKER

REBEL GREEN

PROJECT: Rebel Green DESIGN FIRM: Wink CLIENT: Rebel Green
DESIGNER: Richard Boynton ART DIRECTORS: Richard Boynton, Scott
Thares FONTS USED: Buffet, Bureau Grotesque, Bureau Agency

"Rebel Green is a new breed of responsibly made products. Our charge was to create a brand that's authentic and a product line that was uniquely Eco-Americana, with just a dash of 'you're not the boss of me' thrown in for good measure."

—WINK

FIZZY LIZZY

PROJECT: Fizzy Lizzy Sparkling Juice rebranding **DESIGN FIRM**: Haley
Johnson Design, Inc. **CLIENT**: Fizzy Lizzy LLC **DESIGNER**: Haley
Johnson **PHOTOGRAPHER**: Erin Gleeson **COPYWRITERS**: Haley Johnson, Aaron
Morrill **FONTS USED**: custom

"Fizzy Lizzy is an intense, sparkling fruit juice. The graphics reflect the personality and characteristics of the beverage as well as they reflect the personality and characteristics of Liz herself, the creator of the beverage."

—HALEY JOHNSON DESIGN, INC.

826 VALENCIA

PROJECT: 826 Valencia Pirate Supply Store **DESIGN FIRM:** Office: Jason Schulte Design, Inc. **CLIENT:** 826 Valencia **DESIGNERS:** Jason Schulte, Will Ecke, Gaelyn Mangrum **CREATIVE DIRECTORS:** Jason Schulte, Jill Robertson **PHOTOGRAPHER:** Vanessa Chu **COPYWRITERS:** Dave Eggers, Lisa Pemrick, Jon Adams, Anna Ura, Dan Weiss, Jennifer Traig **FONT USED:** French Speckletone Black

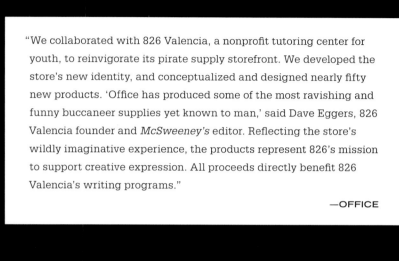

"We collaborated with 826 Valencia, a nonprofit tutoring center for youth, to reinvigorate its pirate supply storefront. We developed the store's new identity, and conceptualized and designed nearly fifty new products. 'Office has produced some of the most ravishing and funny buccaneer supplies yet known to man,' said Dave Eggers, 826 Valencia founder and *McSweeney's* editor. Reflecting the store's wildly imaginative experience, the products represent 826's mission to support creative expression. All proceeds directly benefit 826 Valencia's writing programs."

—OFFICE

TREO

PROJECT: Treo DESIGN FIRM: BVD CLIENT: McNeil GRAPHIC DESIGNER: Bengt Anderung ART DIRECTOR: Rikard Ahlberg CREATIVE DIRECTOR: Catrin Vagnemark FONTS USED: Vectora, modified OL Egyptian

"Our assignment included communicating how easily the tablet dissolves in water, so we worked with a picture of a dissolving tablet. The multitude of small bubbles was a technical challenge, considering the low resolution allowed by the printing techniques."

—BVD

TREO® CITRUS

acetylsalicylsyra, koffein

Lindrar huvudvärk,
annan tillfällig värk och feber.
60 brustabletter (3 rör à 20 st)

Vnr 44 22 28

TREO® COMP

TREO® COMP

acetylsalicylsyra, koffein, kodeinfosfathemihydrat

60 brustabletter (3 rör à 20 st)

Vnr 12 83 97

STEVE'S HOUSE OF CHARM

PROJECT: Steve's House of Charm Le Petit Premiere Collection package **DESIGN FIRM:** Aesthetic Apparatus, Inc. **CLIENT:** Blue Q **DESIGNERS:** Dan Ibarra, Michael Byzewski **ART DIRECTOR:** Mitch Nash **COPYWRITER:** Kelly Lear **INSPIRATIONAL MUSE:** Sara Paul **FONTS USED:** Annabelle, Futura, Futura Display, Futura Condensed, Huxley (modified)

"In some design circles, getting that initial call from Mitch Nash or Deborah Sims at Blue Q is like receiving the Purple Heart. We got our call a few years back and were honored to create a brand that involved the story of a sweet but clueless, quasi-stylish, possibly closeted hairstylist named Steve and his House of Charm beauty parlor. The Steve's House of Charm brand is now employed as a case study of 'the most ingenious, integrated branding system in the world' in many college-level branding textbooks."

—AESTHETIC APPARATUS, INC.

"We were commissioned to create fresh new packaging for a local Dorset cider company. Inspired by English South Coast summer days spent having BBQs and cider by the seaside, the 'Sea Ciders' packaging takes inspiration from all things maritime. Anchors and pirates mix with portholes, crabs and shrimps to create an all-over nautical narrative in this appealing design."

—ILOVEDUST

PROJECT: Sea Cider DESIGN FIRM: ilovedust CLIENT: Hunt Cider Group DESIGNER: Matt Howarth ART DIRECTORS: Mark Graham, Johnny Winslade COPYWRITER: Jill Gate PRINTING: offset litho INKS USED: vegetable based inks PAPER: Robert Horne, cream plus, 740 MIC—fully recyclable and biodegradable FONTS USED: Bespoke, various PRODUCTION TECHNIQUES: Artwork produced on chemical free first generation CTP plates with die cutting

SEA CIDER

THE FARMER IN THE DELI

PROJECT: Farmer in the Deli DESIGN FIRM: Wink CLIENT: Farmer in the Deli DESIGNER: Richard Boynton ART DIRECTORS: Richard Boynton, Scott Thares FONTS USED: Futura, American Typewriter, Clarendon

"The Farmer in the Deli is a line of traditional deli products ranging from sliced meats to potato salad. The identity and packaging system conveys a sense of homemade quality through its classic vernacular that falls somewhere between old recipe cards and vintage metal signs. To keep costs down, the system was essentially comprised of 3-color labels and 1-color paper tape adhered to stock cartons, Ziploc bags and vacuum-sealed meats."

—WINK

THE RUBBER BANDIT

DESIGNER: Andy Mangold **PHOTOGRAPHER:** Andy Mangold
PRINTING TECHNIQUE: Digitally printed on newsprint **FONT USED:**
Archer, in every available weight and style

"This project was a sort of culmination of what was a boyhood obsession of mine of building rubber band guns in my garage. For me, the Rubber Bandit is a marriage between my fun-loving, childish side and the early stages of my professional, 'serious' career as a designer.

I used good old newsprint—the real cheap stuff—because I liked the light tone of grey and wanted the package to age a bit prematurely to emphasize the vintage aesthetic I was going for. I hand-constructed the box and hand-cut the shape of the gun and extra barrels."

—ANDY MANGOLD

the Gentleman's

Rubber Bandit

Solid Wood
Rubber Band Gun

WARNINGS
& PRECAUTIONS

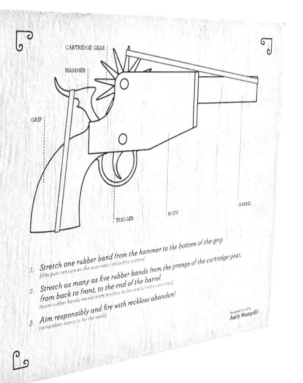

DANGER!

THIS RUBBER BAND GUN, *handcrafted* to the highest standards, IS CAPABLE OF INFLICTING **1st** & **2nd** DEGREE *welts, contusions & bruises* ON THE SUPPLE FLESH OF YOUR TARGETS.

For safety's sake, it should only be weilded by a **TRUSTWORTHY & LICENSED** adult.

For fun's sake, place it in the hands of your CRAZIEST, most **DEMENTED**, **DERANGED, UNBALANCED,** *loose cannon* of a friend & **WATCH THE RUBBER** *fly*.

CARTRIDGE GEAR

HAMMER

GRIP

TRIGGER   BODY   BARREL

1. Stretch one rubber band from the hammer to the bottom of the grip *(this puts tension on the automatic reloading system)*

2. Stretch as many as five rubber bands from the prongs of the cartridge gear, from back to front, to the end of the barrel *(more rubber bands means more tension, be careful not to overload)*

3. Aim responsibly and fire with reckless abandon! *(remember, mercy is for the weak)*

designed & built by **Andy Mangold**

INDEX

PERMISSIONS